The 1

MW01295206

Julius Caesar, Marcus Licinius Crassus, Gnaeus Pompey Magnus, and the fall of the Roman Republic

By Clifford Alexander

Table of Contents

Chapter 1: The Chaotic First Century

The First Triumvirate marks an important demarcation in the development of Roman statehood: it was a time when power became consolidated within the hands of a very few and privileged elite. It was a watershed moment that had tremendous consequences for the future of the Roman dominion. However, it was also a shift in political organization that was long in the making. To thoroughly understand the importance of the First Triumvirate, it is necessary to assess the events and social phenomenon that had preceded it and gripped the Roman Republic. Compared to the second century BC, Rome's entrance into the first century was one of stark contrast to the traditional systems associated with Roman rule. Previously, each member of the state had each a vested interest in maintaining Roman interests at home and abroad. The conflicts of the Punic Wars, or the conquests of Greece and Asia Minor, exemplify this cooperation. The political competition between Roman aristocratic elites fueled her conquests and expansion throughout the Mediterranean.

It is apparent that the first century BC therefore stands apart from preceding centuries as something entirely different: the era of the Roman strongman. It was of the elite, a time when powerful senators — Marius, Sulla, Caesar, and Pompey — all possessed the utmost capability to enact tremendous influence and bind the Roman senate to their will. It was then that elite interests and those of the Roman public effectively became blurred and distorted. The first century is defined by a small group of elites pursuing their own goals under the pretense that they were satisfying the public demands. Many individuals and newcomers to the political realm, such as Julius Caesar, politically aligned themselves as such. The question then becomes one of explaining how such a transition from Republic to oligarchy came about.

Our understanding of this tumultuous period begins in the second century BC: the period that saw the rise of the Roman Republic to its most resplendent position of power. It was then that Rome, through conquest, had carved a place for itself among the great empires of the ancient world. The Second Punic War's conclusion in the dying years of the 3rd century BC brought Rome into its first contact with the Hellenistic kingdoms of Greece and the near East. There, Rome underwent a series of conquests that saw it consuming the former superpowers of the Mediterranean. Rome first overtook the Illyrian kingdoms on the coast of Dalmatia. The pirate menace of the Mediterranean, Illyria proved no match for the fury of the Roman legions.

It became rapidly apparent to the Roman senate that Rome was a military force that had no peer. The Carthaginians, their erstwhile rival, had been defanged and stripped of their military capabilities following the Second Punic War's conclusion in 201 BC. Carthage's subsequent involvement in the Third Punic War (149-146 BC) paled in comparison with their earlier wars with Rome. Whereas previously such conflicts had entailed colossal campaigns that demanded both huge commitments of manpower, the Third Punic War comprised mainly of a token defense of the city of Carthage. This fell to the forces of Scipio Aemilianus in 146 BC.

The Hellenistic kingdoms — derivatives of the earlier conquests by Alexander the Great — could be considered Rome's closest equivalent in terms of power. However, they were militarily inefficient when compared to the Romans. Consisting largely of pike-wielding phalangites, these Hellenistic powers were notoriously rigid when compared to their Italian counterparts. They had become too dependent on the effectiveness of the phalanx – investing the bulk of their resources into hiring mercenaries who had trained in fighting in such a formation. Their strategy was straightforward, pushing their phalanx against the enemy until one side capitulated. This reliance on phalangites was a far cry from the effectiveness of Alexander's army, which employed combined arms in the form of cavalry and skirmishers. Moreover, Alexander was a tactical genius, fixing the enemy body against his phalanx before leading his cavalry to strike at their flanks in a devastating charge. Hellenistic generals, by contrast, merely oversaw the initial formation of their battle line. Rarely did they emulate their illustrious predecessor by partaking in the battle themselves.

Rome's introduction into the Hellenistic world signaled a rupture in the traditional balance of power between Macedon, Ptolemaic Egypt, and the Seleucid Kingdom. First to fall was Philip V and his Kingdom of Macedon, which was immediately punished for its involvement in the Second Punic War. This war, known as the Second Macedonian War, culminated with the battle of Cynoscephalae fought in 197 BC. King Philip's armies were crushed – bringing his involvement in foreign politics to an end. He reigned for the duration of his life in utter fear of future Roman reprisals. Decades later, his successor, King Perseus, attempted to regain Macedon's lost military prestige in what we now call the Third Macedonian War. Perseus' efforts were thwarted at the battle of Pydna in 168 BC, which saw the flexibility of the Roman manipular legion envelop Perseus' rigid phalanx. The Romans, led by the consul Lucius Aemilianus Paulus Macedonicus, took advantage of the battlefield's uneven terrain to pick apart the dense formation of the Macedonian phalangites.

Rome's advance into the Greek world was simultaneously matched with a similar push into Asia. Antiochus III, king of The Seleucid Kingdom of Syria and Asia Minor, eyed the increasing Roman encroachment in Hellenistic affairs with utter disdain. Although eager to attack Rome, Antiochus was prevented by his incessant series of wars in Coele-Syria against Ptolemaic Egypt. His war with Rome would only happen once he had attained a successful peace with his Egyptian enemies, which occurred in 195 BC. His borders with Egypt secured, Antiochus moved against Rome, drawing a number of Greek cities to his banner. These cities were members of the Aetolian League, a confederacy of Greek city-states. The Aetolian League occupied the strategically vital cities of Chalcis and Demetrias in direct contravention to Roman demands. They saw in Antiochus a potential liberator from the tyranny of Rome, and wanted to assist him in any way possible.

Antiochus traversed the Hellespont in 191 BC. His traversal was strikingly similar to that of Xerxes, king of Persia, in 480 BC. Further echoing the distant past was their chosen site for confrontation: Thermopylae, the site of the pyrrhic victory of the Persian army over the Spartan-led Greek coalition. Arriving at Thermopylae, Antiochus met a Roman army under the command of Manius Acilius Glabrio, who manned the hot gates against the oncoming Seleucid threat. The Seleucid army was a mixed army. Partly Hellenistic, it compared to the Macedonian army in that it relied upon a strong corps of pike-wielding phalangites for the majority of its fighting. However, unlike the Macedonian army, the Seleucids had incorporated numerous Eastern influences into its military composition. Its tributary relationship with subjugated Eastern kingdoms had allowed Seleucid armies to employ heavy cataphracts, who, mailed from head-to-toe in armor, wielded maces and axes with which they dealt crushing blows. Antiochus further had a number of scythed chariots. These weapons had long blades that protruded from the wheels, which were devastating to enemy cavalry formations. Lastly, the Seleucids possessed numerous Syrian armored war elephants, which excelled at spreading chaos and disorder among enemy ranks. What was vital for the success of each of these weapons was that they be used in an open field. As Thermopylae was a mountainous range that featured narrow valleys, the Seleucid weapons were unsuitable for use in battle against the Romans. This resulted in Antiochus being forced to depend entirely on his phalanx, whose wall of pikes would have been more than suitable for the narrow causeway of Thermopylae. However, Cato the

Elder describes how Glabrio, under the cover of night, successfully enveloped the Seleucid army by traveling along a remote mountain path to reach the rear of the invaders. When dawn broke, the Romans attacked. What ensued was a general rout of Seleucid forces as the army found itself surrounded by an onslaught of Roman forces on all sides. Pressed, they frantically tried to escape the Roman vice. Contemporary accounts estimate that roughly ten thousand Seleucid soldiers were either killed or captured in the battle. The scale of carnage was amplified by the fact that those who fled had trampled the wounded underfoot. Compared to Antiochus, the Romans only suffered two hundred losses. Among those who fled was Antiochus himself. After the battle, the Seleucid king desperately sought to make peace with the Romans. The Roman demands placed upon him were strict: Antiochus was to surrender his hold on the wealthy dominions in Asia Minor, and promise never to make war with

Rome again. For Antiochus, this was a small sacrifice. Although declining, the Seleucid Kingdom extended still over much of the vast, prosperous dominions of the former Persian Empire. However, to enjoy the fruits of such prosperity, it was necessary that Antiochus become a pawn to the Roman Republic. Without such sacrifices, Antiochus' reign would have been short-lived.

What Rome created in the wake of its victory over Antiochus was a collection of tributary client states in Asia Minor. The Kingdom of Pergamon was one such client state. Its king, Attalus, operated on behalf of Roman interests in the region, carefully monitoring the Asiatic east for any threat to the Republic's dominions. Attalus' grant of the title "friend to the Romans" effectively stabilized Italian commercial interests in the Greek East, and brought a vast influx of wealth into the capital city.

Ptolemaic Egypt remained the final Hellenistic holdout against Roman dominion. However, rather than choosing to capitulate militarily to the Italian power, the Ptolemaic dynasty instead opted to form a tributary relationship with the city of Rome, in which they would supply it with grain on a yearly basis. This was vital for the expansion of the city, whose burgeoning population required an ever-increasing amount of grain to sustain itself.

The Second Century BC: In depth

It is immediately apparent that the second century BC was dominated by the Roman Republic's most glorious conquests. It was a period of near incessant warfare, in which the Roman state expanded out from the Italian peninsula to encompass the majority of the Greek East and Asia Minor. Roman soldiers waged war as far as the coast of the Black Sea, and Roman vessels and trade interests spread further still — creating commercial ties with the civilizations of the Indus Valley. However, the increased conquests and contact that Rome had with other civilizations profoundly changed Roman society. Increased foreign activity further lengthened the wealth disparity that divided the Roman elite from the poor. The lucrative conquests in the East allowed for the Roman elites to accrue a fabulous fortune, as they were the principal beneficiaries of military plunder. On the other hand, the Roman legionnaire — a Roman citizen smallholder — was becoming increasingly impoverished due to the high frequency of military campaigns and the length of time spent on the march. The Roman manipular legion — a military body formed of citizen-soldiers — was differentiated on the basis of class and material wealth, with the sole prerequisite being the possession of land. As the Roman military fought further and further from Italy, Roman legionnaires often spent years in the service. This meant that a Roman citizen had less time to tend to his farm and home, which resulted in many farms falling into disuse.

The stringent requirements created by such a classification were beginning to have a strain on the Roman military by the end of the 2nd century. Some historians posit that the sheer number of wars fought by Rome had the consequence of closing vast numbers of Roman farms, as a result of their proprietor dying or being incapable of operating them. This left them open for purchase up by Italian elites, who began to consolidate such holdings into large plantation estates known as *latifundia*. Tiberius Gracchus, Tribune of the Plebs, was greatly concerned by this development. He famously described how the lands in Campania had become manned entirely by slaves who worked on such *latifundia*. The slaves were abundant in number because of Rome's victorious conquests in the east. These *latifundia* barred poor Romans from possessing farmland of their own. Regardless of the truth of his claims, Gracchus had identified a weakness in the Roman system that had only begun to show due to the pressure created by an influx of slaves. Incapable of owning a farm or working on the *latifundia*, hordes of landless peasants known as *proletarii* flocked to the city of Rome to find work. Their migration from the rural regions of Italy to the city put considerable stress on its grain dole and created instability and civic unrest.

Historians call this event the Gracchan crisis, and both contemporary and modern historians see it as the harbinger for the chaotic unrest that would characterize the first century. Gracchus sought to pass legislation that would protect the Roman poor. He was chiefly concerned with securing the livelihoods of the *proletarii*, but also sought to address the issue of Rome's declining military manpower. Because the Roman legions were manned entirely by landholders, it was worrisome that the number of Roman landholders was declining. If the Gracchan claims were true, they had significant ramifications for Rome's military capabilities. More and more *latifundia* would curb the levying of Roman soldiers tremendously, as slaves were exempted from enlistment in the military. Indeed, what our sources describe is a situation where the Roman military was growing ever more reliant on an increasingly narrow body of citizens for the formation of its legions.

Despite its potential for catastrophe, the Gracchan crisis was never addressed. Instead, Gracchus' attempted reforms triggered a period of Roman political violence — among the first seen since the fall of the Roman kings. For attempting to destroy the *latifundia*, Tiberius Gracchus was murdered in 133 BC. Later, in 121 BC, his brother Gaius attempted to pass what Tiberius had failed to do. However, the fierce senatorial opposition to such reforms ended also with his death. What is evident from these instances is that both deaths occurred at the behest of rival opponents within the Senate. These senators had an interest in maintaining the *latifundia* system of cultivation, as they owned the plantations themselves. However, that such violent measures were resorted to was unprecedented. Both Tiberius and Gaius held the curial office of Tribune, which rendered their person inviolable. Their deaths therefore stood in direct contravention to Roman law. What is apparent is that an increasing malevolence had begun to encroach upon the traditional political system. That no senators were found guilty further demonstrated that violence and murder were feasible alternatives to peaceful discourse.

The reluctance of the Senate to address Gracchus' concerns would have disastrous consequences for the state. By the end of the second century, the wellspring of manpower that Rome had previously enjoyed in earlier conquests was beginning to run dry. This was only realized when two Germanic tribes, the Cimbri and Teutones, began to migrate from their home in the Jutland in 113 BC. Their destination was Italy, and their crossing of the

Alps would result in a series of defeats for the Roman state. Known as the Cimbrian War, the Cimbri and Teutones posed the first serious threat to Roman dominance in Italy since the days of Hannibal and the Second Punic War. The first fires of war emerged around Noricum, after the consul Gnaeus Papirius Carbo was sent to mediate a conflict between the Germanic migrants and those of the Roman-allied Taurisci. Although the consul appealed to diplomatic overtures to pacify the Cimbri and Teutones, he had also attempted to set an ambush to take the Germans by surprise. The Germanic tribes agreed to the consul's demands, but became infuriated upon discovering his ambuscade and attacked. What resulted was a catastrophic Roman defeat at the Battle of Noreia, one from which Carbo only just escaped with his life. The Senate was bewildered by this loss, and tried again and again to subdue the Germanic hordes. What followed were a series of defeats suffered by Rome. The Germanic strategy was erratic. Remaining beyond the periphery of the Alps, they would haphazardly strike at Northern Italian cities. The Romans were surprisingly incapable of addressing this threat, and suffered a significant defeat at Gallia Narbonensis, and another at the Battle of Burdigala. With each successive victory, the Germanic tribes became ever more brazen. They approached many Gallic tribes, inciting them to revolt against their Roman conquerors. The Tigurini, an Alpine tribe, were among these who agreed to unite with the Germans. They defeated a Roman army in 107 BC. Smarted by each defeat, the Senate resolved to end this Germanic invasion from the North.

In 105 BC, they assembled a gargantuan force comprising of two consular armies, which in total numbered over 80,000 men. Gnaeus Mallius Maximus and Quintus Servilius Caepio were appointed to lead this force. However, these men were fierce rivals of one another, and would not cooperate. At the Rhone River, the consuls agreed to pitch camp. However, rather than creating one individual camp, they — divided by their enmity — instead made two separate camps, each comprising a single consular army. In doing so, the Roman force became far weaker by separating their resources in such a manner. Further worsening the situation was the fact that each consul did not respect the other's wishes. Caepio, in a feat of foolishness, led his army out to attack the Germans without waiting for support from Maximus. What followed was a slaughter for Roman forces unseen since the Battle of Cannae during the Second Punic War. Caepio, entirely isolated from Maximus, was powerless as his army was cut down before the Germanic onslaught. Having dealt with Caepio, the Germanic forces then turned to Maximus and besieged his camp. Completely surrounded, Maximus was incapable of mounting a proper defensc and had no hope of being relieved. His forces were promptly cut down in their camp as only a few Romans tried to hold the Germanic tribe at the palisades. The remaining Romans broke and fled, but were picked off by the

German cavalry. Of the 80,000-strong, only a few hundred escaped from the carnage with their lives.

As is evident, these defeats each resulted in a tremendous loss of life for Rome — a catastrophic turn of events for the Roman state during a period where their military manpower reserves were already weakened. The Cimbri and Teutones had successively inflicted defeat after defeat on the Romans – leaving Italy bereft of the forces necessary for an effective defense. Rome's survival at this time was thus secured only by the providence that both the Cimbri and Teutones were preoccupied with finding a home to settle in. This offered the Roman state the opportunity to recuperate from its losses and finally address the issue first enumerated by the Gracchi.

The answer to the question of manpower came from the Roman general and statesman, Gaius Marius. A veteran of the Jugurthine War of 112-106 BC in Numidia, Marius enacted a series of military reforms known as the Marian Reforms. Through them, he eliminated the Roman manipular legion and replaced it instead with the cohorts system of military structure.

The Old Republican Roman Army: In Depth

The Manipular Legion (sometimes called the Polybian Legion in honor of the Greek historian whose account describes it) was the military structure with which the Roman army gained dominance throughout the Mediterranean. Drawn up entirely from Roman citizens, its composition was divided along class lines, and each soldier was expected to provide his own arms and armor. Polybius, writing in the second century BC, provides an extensive description of the Roman army's components in his seminal work, *The Histories*. From this, we conjecture that the traditional Republican legionary formation consisted of four principal divisions. The first division belonged to the skirmishers, known as the *velites*. Lightly armed and armored, the *velites* were usually the youngest or poorest members of the Roman army. Their role was thus limited to light skirmishing with the enemy, which saw them hurl javelins among the enemy ranks, or accompany the Roman cavalry on scouting exercises. Contemporary accounts describe that some *velites* would even emblazon their armor with animal furs or vivid cloths so that their peers could better witness their individual feats of martial glory.

Following the *velites* came the core divisions of heavy infantry, formed in ranks known as the *triplex acies*. Within this formation, each progressive rank was formed of heavier and heavier infantry. The first rank was formed of soldiers known as *hastati. Hastati* were better armed and armored than the *velites,* and sported bronze breastplates and long shields. They were responsible for much of the fighting following first contact with the enemy. Each individual *hastati* belonged to a greater group of eighty men, known as a century. Prior to forming a battle line, these individual centuries would march apart, providing space for the *velites* to retreat through their ranks following the conclusion of skirmishing. Every *hastati* possessed both a short sword known as a *gladius*, and a throwing spear called a *pilum*. These *pila* were thrown in an attempt to break apart a dense enemy formation and render their shields unusable.

The *hastati* would fight for some time, softening up the enemy ranks before being relieved by the more heavily armed and armored *principes*. The *principes* had both greater seniority than the *hastati,* and greater wealth, and thus could afford to purchase better protection. These were the effective shock troops of the Roman Republican army: charging when the enemy was exhausted and already engaged with the *hastati*. They used their combined weight to create a ferocious onslaught capable of breaking both their enemies' ranks and their will.

The *principes* therefore had a greater responsibility on the battlefield when compared to the *hastati* and *velites,* but also were far more experienced as a result.

The final rank of the *triplex acies* belonged to the *triarii*, the oldest and most experienced troops in the legion. These soldiers were armed and armored in a wholly different way from the previous units. Rather than swords and *pilum*, they wielded long stabbing spears, and were extremely armored. The *triarii* represent a holdover from a bygone period in Roman warfare history. It is believed that the *triarii* fought in a manner more akin to a Greek hoplite than a Roman legionary — fighting in a dense, inelastic formation similar to a phalanx, and being used only as a last resort when the battle was at its most dire.

The last component of the Roman army was the cavalry, deriving entirely from the *equites* class of the citizen body. These were the wealthiest members of the plebeian caste, and as such could afford to maintain both a stable and a horse. Despite their wealth requirements, the Roman cavalry was famously ineffective. This is likely due to the ruggedness of the central Italian terrain, which did not provide an adequate roaming area for horse herds. Nor was equestrianism a particularly important skill in ancient Rome. The horse cultures of the Asian steppes or even the Gallic tribes of France had better cavalry, because of their reliance on horses to generate their livelihoods.

The Marian Reforms: Consequences for Roman Statehood

The Marian Reforms signaled a tremendous change for the structure of the Roman military. Gone were the rigid landholding requirements and class divisions that had previously characterized the earlier Republican army. Instead, any and all landless inhabitants were welcomed into the military. These individuals no longer had to shoulder the expense of arming themselves, and instead were financed from the state purse. There is a degree of speculation as to how extensively these reforms were applied, and some historians posit that legionaries were still responsible for paying for armament replacements, such as spare shields, *gladii*, or *pila*. These reforms changed the minimum amount of time spent in the military, increasing the duration of service to 25 years. After this length of time had elapsed, soldiers were rewarded for their service with allotments of land in the form of veteran's colonies. Marius' reformation effectively shifted the core of the Roman army, changing it from one composed entirely of militia to one that was professional. Under his guidance, its ranks were now made up entirely of career soldiers who knew nothing more than conquest and warring. The Marian Legion was thus designed entirely around heavy infantry, and was manned by members of the lowest classes in Roman society. By arming these men from the state purse, the reformation was a phenomenal success: creating a sizable army out of the horde of landless citizens in Rome. On the other hand, these lower class individuals had no political connections unlike their elite counterparts, and thus their closest link to the Roman senate was through their general.

The Marian Reforms presented a watershed in the functionality of the Roman army. However, there existed one glaring flaw in its composition. Although the army was entirely state-run and financed, it had altogether no reason for loyalty to the Roman Senate. This was due to the veteran's allotments that were administered as rewards for service upon retirement. The Roman Senate had not been successful in designing a system that would equally grant land to each individual soldier upon retirement. Instead they left it as the responsibility of each general following a campaign. What had been but a minor bureaucratic inconvenience at the time would end up creating tremendous problems in the following years. By not monopolizing the allocation of veteran's colonies following termination of service, the Senate had in actuality made their legionaries fiercely loyal to the general, and him alone. This exclusion of the Roman senate would have disastrous repercussions, rendering the state captive to the demands of the armies it fielded.

Thus, the formation for the era of the powerful Roman strongman was materialized. Unfettered by ties to the state, and armed with the support of powerful, veteran legionary armies, Roman elites were now capable of intimidating the Roman senate into fulfilling their desires. These reformations were to signal the commencement of a bloody and chaotic period in Roman history. The catalyst for the commencement of such conflict took the form of a Roman politician by the name of Lucius Cornelius Sulla.

Sulla: The Social War

Lucius Cornelius Sulla emerged onto the political stage from a backdrop of violence and domestic instability known as the Social War of 91 BC: a brutal civil war that would shock and temporarily rupture the very fabric of the Roman state. The Social War pitted Rome against its former Italian allies. Their cause for revolt was due to their status as citizens. Many Italian allies had borne the costs of Rome's military conquests and fought alongside Roman troops across the span of the Mediterranean. However, despite these achievements, the Italians continued to be considered second-class citizens. In spite of the repeated requests, the Roman senate continued to deny the extension of Roman citizenship to the allies.

The conflict would flare in 91 BC with the assassination of the then Tribune of the Plebs, Marcus Livius Drusus. Drusus had aspired to extend the right of Roman citizenship to the Italian allies by appealing to both the Senate and the equestrian order. He had hoped to win popular support by expanding the size of the Senate house, and also reviving investigations into charges of bribery. However, this succeeded only in uniting both the equestrians and the senators against Drusus, who each had their own reasons as to preventing such investigations into corruption. Some senators were also aware that if Drusus were successful in extending the franchise, his gain in political influence would have been considerable, as countless Italian elites would have then become his clients. These Italians were frustrated by the senate's repeated objection to their grant of franchise, and so were willing to ally with anyone who lent them a sympathetic ear. Drusus' death, therefore, triggered malevolence among the Italians. In reaction, they sent embassies among themselves, forming secret alliances that united the Italian communities against Rome. The Roman historian, Appian, writes that the state was long ignorant of this hostile intrigue. Gradually, details of the conspiracy came to light, and the Roman Senate sent a number of ambassadors to suspect Italian communities. Their mission was to investigate if there were any truth to these claims.

It was at Asculum that the Social War began. The Roman ambassadors sent there were taken hostage and executed by its inhabitants. The events at Asculum catalyzed the greater Italian revolt, whereby Italian communities declared their independence from Rome, and proclaimed the formation of their own state, Italica. The Italians were so committed to their revolution that they had new coins minted to celebrate their newfound nation. This presented an incredibly troubling scenario for the Romans: the Italian states had always contributed soldiers to Rome's wars, which deprived the senate of nearly half of its manpower. Moreover, the Italian armies were composed of veterans who had served in Roman campaigns, thereby making them highly trained and disciplined. Lastly, many Romans were upset and demoralized at the idea of fighting former friends and allies. There exist accounts of many Roman and Italians recognizing former friends amidst the opposing battle lines. Popular opinion in Rome was divided on the issue. The Social War was no petty revolt: it was the first case of true civil war in the Republic where one can say that Roman fought against Roman. The scale of the fighting was so intense, and the battles so bloody, that the Roman senate hastily made concessions to the Italians. They were to be given the full citizenship.

Central in bringing about a resolution to the conflict were the efforts of Sulla, who had been elected by the Roman Senate to lead its armies into battle. This decision was made out of fear: the Senate was long suspicious of Marius, having appointed him to the consulship five times out of six. They were wary that Marius might grow too powerful; too beloved by the Roman people. By appointing Sulla, the Senate hoped to balance Marius' success and offer another official the chance to win fame and glory

— to effectively check the former general. Sulla was successful in stemming the outbreaks of the Italian revolts. Under his direction, the Romans were capable of defeating the Italians by 89 BC. Scarred by the Social War, the senate's goal in granting the Roman franchise was preventative. They wanted to mitigate the possibility for any future conflict between the Italian communities and Rome.

While Rome was embroiled in the midst of the Social War, Mithridates VI, the king of Pontus — a nation in Asia Minor — struck out against the Roman communities along the Asiatic coast. He began with Rome's client, the kingdom of Pergamon. Mithridates knew that the Social War had left Rome in a state of weakness, and struck out in a series of conquests in Asia Minor. He was hugely successful. Like his Hellenistic predecessors, Mithridates proclaimed himself as the liberator of all Greeks, and took advantage of the growing resentment felt towards Rome on the part of the local Greek communities. Many were upset at the treatment they had received under Roman rule, as the Roman debt collectors — known as *publicanii* — were committing flagrant abuses of power. The *publicanii* operated with impunity, taking those Greeks who could not repay their debts into slavery as remuneration for past debts. With Mithridates' goading, the Greek population of Asia Minor turned against their Roman neighbors in 88 BC. What followed was a widespread slaughter of thousands of "Romans" throughout the Anatolian region — a surprising number, when we consider that the Romans had only first officially encroached into the region with their wars against Antiochus III and the Seleucids. It is telling of the degree of commercial integration of much of the Roman Empire, as many of these Romans would have been merchants and their families. Moreover, it is possible that at this point in time, the Greeks had grouped the Romans and Italians residing abroad East under one heading: Romans. This is perhaps why the Italians were so frustrated prior to the Social War: treated as Romans abroad, they had to return to their status as second-class citizens upon their return home.

Mithridates VI massacres succeeded in convincing hundreds of Greek communities to join his cause. Among their number was Athens, the former staunch ally of Rome The Social War's conclusion in 88 BC allowed the Senate to focus its attention on halting Mithridates' advance throughout Asia and Greece. To address the mounting conflict in the East, the Senate again appointed Sulla to lead its armies, granting him a sizeable invasion force with which to dislodge the Pontic armies from Greece. However, Sulla was drawn in two directions. Although events in Greece demanded his attention, events in Rome were far more troubling. The retired Marius desired a command in Asia Minor so that he might campaign against Mithridates. To achieve this appointment, he had allied himself with Sulla's enemy, Publius Sulpicius Rufus. Rufus sought to reorganize the nature of the Italian involvement within the Roman military. By lending his support, Marius had effectively emboldened Sulpicius to challenge Sulla's reputation, and he began to push forward his own pro-Italian legislation. These developments were of great concern to Sulla, prompting him to personally depart from the Roman siege of Nola. Unfortunately, Sulpicius' supporters fiercely contested his arrival in Rome, and he found himself forced to seek refuge from the mob inside the house of Marius. Caught in Sulpicius' trap, Sulla was pressured with threats of looming violence to consent to the former's legislation.

Although victorious, Sulpicius was apprehensive of Sulla's return to the Greek war, and was doubly pressured to remove the latter from his command by Marius. By promising to wipe his debts free, Marius won Sulpicius' support, and convinced the latter to form an Assembly of the People with the goal of removing Sulla from his command of the Mithridatic campaign. This decision was met with tremendous hostility in Rome: Sulla's supporters rioted throughout the city, but were prevented from killing Sulpicius by his ring of armed bodyguards. Sulla learned of the news while encamped and preparing to embark for Greece with his most loyal legions, and vowed to march on Rome to right what he believed to be a perversion of the Roman constitution. His march was swift, and brutal — standing in clear violation of the ancient law of the *pomerium*, which forbade any Roman army from entering within the vicinity of Rome while under command of a consul. Sulla's opponents were punished severely for their flagrant attacks against him, and Marius himself hastened desperately to amass some form of army to meet Sulla — promising any slave his freedom in exchange for service. However, Marius' supporters were so few that he was forced to flee the city. He abandoned Rome to Sulla, and departed for Africa, where he still enjoyed support for his successes in the earlier Jugurthine War.

Empowered by the proximity of his legions, Sulla addressed the Senate in harsh tones, justifying his march on Rome by the fact that the Senate had violated the law of *mos maiorum,* which protected the consuls' rights to individual campaigns. He declared a proscription against Marius and his supporters, branding them as enemies of the state. Proscribed, their right to property was declared void and their lives were forfeit. Labeled an enemy, Sulpicius was betrayed and murdered by his slave, whom Sulla later freed to summarily execute. Content with the reinforcement of his position in Rome, Sulla departed again for Greece. He vowed to bring the Mithridatic War to a close.

Marius was not content to sit idly by while Sulla reigned supreme. He resolved to return to Rome and hold the consulship for a seventh time — regardless of whatever costs it might entail. Marius made careful overtures to whatever supporters he still possessed in Rome, allying himself with a leading politician by the name of Cinna. Satisfied with the existence of a sufficient powerbase in Rome, Marius returned to Rome in the following spring and declared Sulla's legal reformations invalid. He lifted the proscription off of his supporters, and instead declared the city in open hostility towards Sulla. In a final gesture, Marius exiled Sulla, and then assumed the consulship alongside Cinna. Marius' death a fortnight later left Cinna as sole consul, and deprived him from the broad powerbase he had only so recently enjoyed.

The Mithridatic War commanded the attention of Sulla from the years 87 BC to 85 BC. However, he remained ever mindful of events in the city of Rome. Due to Marius, his legions and supporters were now all exiled from Rome — making them a rogue Roman army fighting Mithridates in Greece. Sulla's victory over Mithridates, first at Athens, and then at Chaeoroneia and Orchomenus, allowed for the possibility of negotiations with the Pontic king. It was agreed that Mithridates would pay an immense war indemnity to the Roman populace for his belligerence and violation of their trust. Furthermore, he would have to surrender a sizable portion of his dominion. In return for his compliance with Sulla's demands, Mithridates would have his title of friend of the Romans returned to him, and would be allowed to continue to peacefully reign over his kingdom.

The conclusion of the Mithridatic War did not entail the end of conflict in Asia, however. Mithridates' efforts, and the weakening of Roman influence in the region had wrought chaos and lawlessness. Even the Romans were not immune to the pull of gold. The opportunity for plundering and pillaging proved too appealing to ignore for some of the legions serving alongside Sulla, which prompted a small rebellion under the command of legate Gaius Flavius Fimbria. Fimbria and his men broke from the leadership of Sulla's second in command, Lucius Valerius Flaccus. They occupied the city of Byzantium on the Hellespont. Flaccus attempted to bring a halt to this rebellion, but was instead betrayed and mutinied by his own troops, who preferred Fimbria's leniency regarding the accumulation of plunder. Fimbria, now in complete command of Flaccus' former army, operated under the pretence that he was working alongside Sulla, but was in actuality working against his interests. Fimbria, incapable of resuming conflict with Mithridates, turned instead to Asia and proceeded to attack not only Greek enemies, but also Sulla's allies, as well. Sulla, aware that the situation back in Rome was growing evermore dire, pressed the issue and cornered Fimbria in his winter camp in the Cappadocian hills. Fimbria's troops, aware that they were now facing Sulla and his legions, defected to his army *en masse*. Fimbria, in utter despair, committed suicide rather than face his former commander's wrath.

Aware of the grievances in his army, Sulla allowed his soldier's to satisfy their need for wealth and plunder. His legions wantonly pillaged the cities of the Ionian coast on their return to Rome in 84 BC. His justification for permitting such acts was simple: the plunder was compensation for the years of taxation lost by the Greek revolt. Cinna, still consul in Rome, was alarmed by reports of Sulla's return to Italy, and began to assemble an army to thwart his attempt. While marching over the Apennines towards Illyria, however, Cinna was faced with a large mutiny among his officers — who had him flogged to death. Desperate now, the Senate attempted to raise two more armies in 83 BC, one under the consul Gaius Norbanus, and the other headed by his colleague, L. Cornelius Scipio Asiagenus. Norbanus' army attempted to bar the passing of Sulla at Canusium, but was defeated and forced back to Capua. This offered no respite — Sulla followed right on Norbanus' heels. The second army, under Asiagenus, sought to face Sulla in the south of Italy, where it could earn the support of local Italian communities. Despite this maneuver, Asiagenus' army quickly abandoned him; perhaps due to the machinations of Sulla's agents or the terrifying reputation of his battle-hardened veterans. Drawing negotiations between himself and Sulla, Asiagenus entreated his opponent to spare his life, which the latter consented to only if he swore allegiance to his cause. This Asiagenus readily agreed to. However, once free, Asiagenus quickly rescinded his support for Sulla — calling the latter a tyrant. In the wake of this betrayal, Sulla would no longer be lenient towards his enemies.

It rapidly became evident to the elites of Italy that Sulla would be victorious in his march on Rome — that the three victories he had won against Roman armies were not accomplished by chance alone. As a result, Roman elites flocked to his banner. Quintus Caecilius Metellus was the first to declare his allegiance, ousting supporters of Marius from North Africa. Marcus Licinius Crassus brought his armies from Spain to support Sulla. Pompeius Strabo's son, later to be known as Gnaeus Pompey Magnus, also declared his loyalty for Sulla and raised an army of his own.

The situation looked dire for Asiagenus — Italy was rapidly turning its back on the Roman senate. They needed a victory, and fast. He chose to strike out at the most inexperienced of Sulla's lieutenants, that being Pompey Magnus, who was winning over Italian cities in Northern Italy. However, just as before, Asiagenus' soldiers defected over to Sulla at the earliest opportunity. Asiagenus, under proscription and now bereft of an army, had little choice but to flee to Masillia, where he would live the remainder of his life.

Now devoid of an army and any competent commanders, the Roman Senate turned to the name of Marius in an effort to rally support. They appointed his son, Gaius Marius the Younger, to the consulship at the young age of 26. Such an appointment was exceedingly rare — most consuls being selected in their 40s and 50s. Hoping to prevent the desertions of the past, they also selected to recruit from among the most loyal Italian communities. This was an easy accomplishment: there was no love between Italians and Sulla. Many Samnite communities — erstwhile staunch opponents to Roman rule — flocked to the banner of Marius and the Senate. A series of indecisive battles were fought between Sulla and the senate's armies, with a gradual attrition taxing at the strength of the pro-senate forces, as their generals either fled or were betrayed by their soldiers. Sulla's appeal was incomparable.

In 82 BC, the conflict came to a head at the Colline Gates outside of the city of Rome. There, the armies of Sulla, supported by Pompey Magnus and Crassus, met the Samnite armies of Marius. Both sides were convinced of the righteousness of their cause, each believing themselves to be preserving the Roman state. It was a fiercely fought battle: the Samnite divisions that composed Marius army being equally as experienced as their Roman counterparts. They pressed hard against Sulla's legions, pushing him to the very gates of Rome itself. It was only with Crassus' offensive that Sulla succeeded in overturning his enemy's flank, and was capable of routing the Marian army. Abandoned by his soldiers, Marius the Younger committed suicide. Rome was Sulla's for the taking.

Sulla's reign over the city of Rome represented the first instance of Rome transitioning from Republic to a monarchic form of government. His first act was to revive the ancient office of dictator, which had not been used since the desperate days of the Second Punic War. The dictatorship conferred emergency powers upon whoever held the office, allowing them to effectively override any appeals from the senate. It was originally designed to act as a flexible alternative to the rigid legislative processes of the senate, and was therefore only appointed during times of great crisis. As a result, the Dictator had the privilege of absolute power — a rarity in the Roman system. The Assembly of the People ratified Sulla's decision to assume the dictatorship, and placed no limit on the length of time he would spend in office. Using the Marian Wars as pretext, Sulla then wielded the role to enact a wide-ranging degree of changes to the Roman state. Most infamous of these were his proscriptions, with which he deemed his opponents enemies of the state. Proscribed, it became the solemn duty of all Romans to do harm to these enemies of the state: to deprive them of their property, and kill them where possible. Helping or assisting any proscribed enemy was equally punishable by death. Should someone kill a proscribed person, they were to be rewarded with a bounty of two talents — a significant sum. Such an incentive pitted slave against master, husband against wife, brother against brother.

Unlike previous instances enacted by Marius and Cinna, Sulla did not limit the extent of his proscriptions to an isolated few. Instead, he stretched the capital punishment to encompass even those whom his allies had deemed enemies, killing any potential opponent until the streets of Rome ran with the blood of his enemies. Many of those killed did not pose a significant threat to Sulla. However, they did possess property that Sulla or his supporters desired. Through strength in numbers and arms, Sulla's rein of terror saw many homes and estates switch hands, as property was seized and auctioned off for a tremendous profit. Lastly, as a final precaution, Sulla extended the effects of proscription to the progeny of those proscribed. Under this decree, the sons and grandsons of his victims were prevented from standing for state office. Perhaps most interesting was Sulla's proscription of Julius Caesar, who was related to Cinna by marriage. Sulla remarked that Caesar's vain ambition posed a threat to the wellbeing of the Roman state. Caesar was only spared Sulla's wrath through the efforts of his *Julii* relatives who had staunchly supported Sulla in his war with Marius. Sulla would later remark that he regretted sparing Caesar's life — seeing in his eyes the making of another Marius.

Sulla belonged to the *optimates*, in that he believed that power should remain in the hands of the traditional, established elite. As such, he sought to weaken the capabilities of the Assembly of the People, who previously had attempted to usurp his consulship and command in the East. He reinstituted his earlier reforms that required that a majority within the senate to ratify each bill passed. Sulla further weakened the plebeian caste by removing the legislative capabilities of the Tribunes. An ardent patrician, he believed the Tribunal office had created nothing but chaos for the Roman state. He further weakened the plebcian caste by barring Tribunes from holding future curial offices. This discouraged aspiring plebeian elites from pursuing the office of Tribune of the Plebs.

Lastly, he removed the power of veto that the Tribune had traditionally enjoyed — thus preventing them from impeding on the passing of pro-Senate legislation. Under Sulla, the office of Tribune and the overt influence of the plebeian caste were reduced to near nothingness.

Sulla further strengthened the Senate by increasing its number from 300 to 600. This effectively flooded the Senate House — the *Curia Hostilia* — with Sulla's supporters, as Sulla appointed new senators from among the ranks of his most loyal supporters. He also transferred control of the courts from the equestrian class to the Senate — further weakening the plebeian caste, and increasing the grandeur of the patricians. These were ambitious gestures: Sulla consolidated legislative and judicial power within the hands of a Senate that was subservient to his will.

His most important reform as dictator was to solidify the requirements for Roman curial office. In doing so, Sulla effectively sought to prevent another general from seizing power in the same way he himself had gained it. As such, he reinstated the minimum requirement that ten-years elapse until an individual became eligible for another consulship. This was designed to prevent a situation like that of Marius, who had held the consulship seven times throughout his political career. This is telling of Sulla's thinking, in that he himself recognized that men with great reputations posed a threat to Rome's future stability.

Lastly, Sulla extended the boundaries of the *pomerium*: the sacred line that barred Roman consuls from entering Rome while possessing *imperium*. This was unprecedented, as the *pomerium* had existed in its previous location since the days of the Roman kings. It was a calculated act on the part of Sulla, designed to demonstrate the breadth of his power and influence in the Roman Senate.

Content with his reforms and changes, Sulla stepped down from his dictatorship in 81

BC, and ran for consul in the subsequent year. Unsurprisingly, he won unanimous support. His retirement from public life in 79 BC was spent in peace, where he wrote his memoirs, which were completed prior to his death in the following year.

Although masquerading as a traditionalist, Sulla had successfully ruptured the traditional framework of the Roman state. By attempting to stabilize Rome's domestic political situation, Sulla had effectively consolidated power within one branch of its government: the Senate. This would have vast consequences for the plebeians, who were accustomed to enjoying some degree of legislative power through the Tribune. Moreover, his march on Rome had effectively set a dangerous precedent: he had demonstrated that it was possible for a Roman general to use the State's legions to seize power. Members of both the First and Second Triumvirates would later emulate such a gesture in the following decades. However, despite his sweeping reforms, Sulla had failed to recognize where the true danger lay: the soldiers. His preoccupation with preventing the rise of another Marius had led to this oversight. Although he had recognized the proper symptoms of the Roman *malaise*, he had not sufficiently identified the associated illness that plagued the Roman state: that the legions remained loyal to their generals, but not the state. Such a lapse would allow for the possibility of future domestic strife in Rome. Such conflict would come about only twenty years following Sulla, with the rise of the First Triumvirate.

Chapter 2: Elite Politics in the Late Republic BC

With the historical precedent established by Sulla, it was inevitable that others might seek to emulate his actions and achieve both power and prestige through illegal means. Sulla's success in achieving Rome's most illustrious offices demonstrated that violence against the Roman State could secure one a place amongst its greatest. Although he attempted to prevent others from repeating his successes, the mechanisms by which Sulla had gained power remained glaringly in place.

Come 60 BC, many of Sulla's supporters had achieved a degree of political success on their own accord. Chief of these were Marcus Licinius Crassus and Gnaeus Pompeius Magnus. Both had earned their fortunes and political favors leading armies on Sulla's behalf twenty years earlier. Since then, they had amassed considerable wealth and influence, and created significant political connections both at home in Italy and abroad.

The Roman Political System: Social Network Ties

At its most fundamental level, Republican politics in Rome were defined by one's proximity to the Senate. If one wished to enact legislative change or direct external investment to one's community, one needed to travel to Rome itself and appeal before the Senate in person. This was problematic for a number of reasons. First and foremost, the Senate was a closed organization, and appeals would be permitted only on an invitational basis. Polybius describes many accounts of Greek diplomats waiting months on end —even years — for an audience with the Senate. Second, many local elites within Italian communities could not afford to take the time or risk the danger inherent when traveling to Rome. The alternative to resolving this predicament was to confer influence upon oneself, and create ties and alliances with powerful individuals in Rome — often important friends and contacts within the Senate itself. These elite social networks stretched far and wide across Italy, and were founded on the principal of *hospitium*, or "guest-friendship." Many of these ties had existed between elite families for centuries, their permanence evidenced by the existence of bronze sculptures dedicated to commemorating such friendships.

These ties of *hospitium* provided the very foundation for political power in Rome. The more individuals a patrician added to his *clientele*, the more magnificent and capable he appeared in the eyes of his colleagues. The Roman morning address known as the *salutatio* was designed to illustrate this power dynamic. Every morning, Roman patricians held a meeting in their central atrium, during which petitioning clients came to offer news and beseech requests. There, each client was subject to a monumental display of the patrician's achievements. The structure of a patrician's home was oriented to display spoils of conquest, rare gifts, emblems of guest friendship, and other symbols of power. The very purpose of this was to impress — to communicate the message that he was a man who had previously accomplished great things, and would continue to do so. This had a central role in the brokering of the Roman power dynamic. Highly competitive, Roman elites sought to portray themselves as greatly capable and affluent so as to attract more clients to their fold. By doing so, most patricians benefited through the increased political support that a client provided. Such an example is illustrated by Drusus' attempt to grant Roman citizenship to the Italian allies prior to the Social War. In granting the franchise, Drusus would have effectively created a new branch of senators, as the wealthiest Italians joined the patrician caste. Moreover, clients would guarantee the preservation of a patrician's trade interests at home and abroad. Many senators were directly banned from participating in trade themselves, but many continued to expand on their fortunes by operating through third-party intermediaries. Lastly, clients offered senators military support in the form of levying troops to serve on their behalf. These local elites had great influence within their local communities, and therefore would help direct their communities towards supporting one side over another during the ensuing Roman Civil Wars of the first century. In exchange, the patrons would assist in enfranchising communities by working towards earning them Roman citizenship, or even invest money into creating new buildings in their communities. Acts of euergetism (doing good deeds characterized by building public works, monumental structures, and infrastructure) are well demonstrated across the Roman world, as wealthy Roman elites rewarded communities for their loyalty by constructing for them buildings and aqueducts. These structures each carried the name of their benefactor, and thus continued to broadcast his power and affluence.

Such was the reciprocal nature of the Roman power dynamic. Through social networks and ties of *hospitium*, no good deed went unrewarded. The advent of this relationship was further enabled by the influx of wealth and precious goods from the Asiatic conquests in the latter half of the second and early first centuries BC. These connections allowed for the creation of veritable strongholds: bastions of power from which Roman elites could depend on for support in their endeavors. One such area was the province of Cisalpine Gaul in Northern Italy, which had been denied the franchise for much of Republican Roman history, despite being populated by Roman colonists. Although formerly Roman citizens, these colonists had lost their franchise as their communities were founded on what was formerly Celtic territory. This resulted in them possessing only the *socii* franchise, or Allied Right. Frustrated, many of these Northern Italian cities joined the cause of the Italians during the Social War — fighting against their former fellow Romans.

Much to their disappointment, the grants of franchise that concluded the Social War did not result with these Northern Italian cities gaining Roman citizenship. This blatant dismissal by the Senate compounded the bitterness already felt by Cisalpine Gaul towards Rome. However, what this setback created was a tremendous opportunity for an aspiring senator. Pompey Strabo, the father of Pompey Magnus, spied the potential for accruing a strong powerbase in the region. His law of 89 BC, known as the *Lex Pompeia de Transpadanis* extended the Latin franchise to these cities beyond the Po River. Although not the full Roman franchise, the Latin Right was an improved condition over their status as Allies. Moreover, the Latin Right allowed magistrates of these cities to obtain Roman citizenship by serving in local office. As thanks for the legislation, these cities are reported by Cicero to have been serving Strabo — and later, Magnus' — interests well into the First Triumvirate.

A Roman senator therefore operated not solely for his own interests, but also for those of his clients. Within the Senate, there also existed an allegiance to a greater club, or political grouping. Formed of likeminded men, these clubs were more of a common alliance than an actual political party. These divisions fragmented the *optimates* from the *populares*. The *optimates* represented the traditional aristocracy of the Republic. They were lauded, venerable elites who had lineages that stretched back to the days of the Roman kings. They were ardent conservatives: looking to protect their own interests, and were wary of those who might excite the public sentiment towards gestures of revolution. In opposition to them were the *populares*, a much smaller subset of the Senate. The *populares* were largely composed of "new men" — newer senators who lacked the pedigree enjoyed by their colleagues. As political influence relied on lineage and reputation as much as wealth, these new men were often alienated from the political system. These men were often only capable of earning a name by becoming a client of an already established patron. Most sought their political leverage through popular support. Known as *populares*, these patricians employed fiery rhetoric to inflame the public sentiment and appeal to popular approval to sway and influence the Senate. Given their nature, the two groups were often opposed to one another.

Although grouped separately, these classifications were not as dichotomizing as they pretended to be. Many senators found themselves often resorting to either appeals to the people or an appeal to the traditional aristocracy to pass their legislation. Unlike modern democratic politics, which foster cooperation between members who shared similar ideas, the *populares* and *optimates* worked just as much against each other as in support for one another.

<u>Crassus & Pompey</u>

As we have seen, Marcus Licinius Crassus and Gnaeus Pompey Magnus had both began their political careers during the Marian Wars. There they served Sulla, assisting him in his victory over the Roman Senate. Each had played a role in the defeat of both of the armies of Scipio Asiagenus and Gaius Marius the Younger. Crassus himself was well rewarded by Sulla for his impressive performance in defeating Gaius Marius the Younger at the battle of the Colline Gates in 82 BC. By contrast, Pompey had previously earned his first victories against Asiagenus in Northern Italy. Having been the subject of such acclaim at a young age, it was inevitable that both men would have a pivotal role in the development of the mid-century.

<u>Gnaeus Pompey "The Great"</u>

Gnaeus Pompey Magnus was the son of Gnaeus Pompey Strabo, a wealthy Italian who had been the first to establish a place for his family among the Roman nobility. Being a new man from Picenum, Pompey Strabo had acquired a reputation for licentiousness, double-dealings, and betrayal. He strove to build a following among the Northern Italian cities in Cisalpine Gaul, which he accomplished in 89 BC with his *Lex Pompedeia*. This law granted the cities the Latin Right. Using these cities as support, contemporary sources argued that Pompey hoped to build a much larger network throughout Cisalpine Gaul and much of Samnium. His death in 87 BC during the Marian War ended such designs.

Gnaeus Pompey Magnus was the beneficiary of his father's demise, inheriting his lands, title, and the loyalty of his father's legions. With these soldiers in tow, Gnaeus Pompey Magnus declared himself openly for Sulla at age 23. The Roman general Asiagenus hoped to easily defeat the young Pompey in Northern Italy, but was abandoned by his own soldiers prior to battle. Pompey Magnus would continue to have a significant role in the Marian War, winning a number of victories for Sulla, which earned him the title of "Conqueror." Pompey's loyalty to Sulla was again reaffirmed through a marriage to the latter's daughter, Aemillia, which only ended when she died in childbirth. Despite her premature death, Pompey continued to enjoy political favor, and was the recipient of great military commands. He was appointed the leader of Sulla's forces in Marian North Africa and Sicily, pushing the forces of Gnaeus Papirius Carbo from the island, and securing Rome's grain supply. In North Africa, he defeated both Gnaeus Domitius Ahenobarbus, and his Numidian ally, King Hiarbas. His swift military success made Sulla apprehensive of Pompey, who had not yet come to possess any curial offices of his own. Regardless, Sulla bequeathed upon him the cognomen Magnus — "The Great" — for his successes abroad. This did little to cool Pompey's famous bigheadedness, as he began to demand his own triumphal procession for his efforts in North Africa. Sulla was hesitant. Such an event was only given to the greatest of Rome's heroes — those who had commanded great armies and fielded extraordinary victories. After some time, he consented, and gave Magnus his position in the triumphal procession: third, after Sulla and Metellus Pius — victorious against Sertorius, the Marian general in Spain. Such a gesture could be only interpreted as Sulla putting Magnus in his place.

That is not to say that Pompey was entirely self-centered. He was merely aware of his place in the Roman constellation. Pompey knew that political acumen predominately derived from one's reputation, and was thus looking for every opportunity to showcase his successes before the city of Rome. Triumphal processions for military victories offered him such a chance, and created within the city an almost legendary following. His soldiers had their own misgivings about their general. Although Pompey commanded their respect, he had not earned their love. Pompey stood calmly when his soldiers threatened to mutiny prior to the triumphal procession. They were upset at being denied their fair share of plunder from the African campaign. Pompey's blatant disregard for their wellbeing cowed them from revolting.

Pompey believed that the traditional rules that defined the curial roster did not apply to him. He was motivated by military glory, and sought new opportunities to further enhance his burgeoning reputation and expand his influence. As such, when the Roman Senate was tasked with raising an army to contend with Quintus Sertorius' continued revolt in Spain, Pompey resolved to obtain it. The senators, however, were mindful of the ambitious Pompey, and feared that his successes would turn him into another Sulla. They denied his request to fight in Spain. Faced with this rejection, Pompey did not disappoint the Senate's prediction. Emulating Sulla, Pompey refused to disband his legions until they had conferred upon him the command in Spain. The senators acceded.

The conflict in Spain stretched from 76-71 BC, prolonged as it was by Sertorius' growing reliance on guerilla tactics. Gradually, Pompey won successive victories against Sertorius' junior officers, which set momentum pushing against his Marian enemy. Attrition gripped the Marian army, and slowly Sertorius' holdings were limited to the province of Lusitania on the Atlantic coast. The conflict came to a conclusion when Sertorius' own officer, Marcus Perperna Vento, murdered him to take command of his army. Under Vento's leadership, the Marian forces engaged Pompey in open battle, only to suffer a crushing defeat.

The beginning of the year 71 marked the end of the Spanish revolt, bringing with it another successful campaign to add to Pompey's growing list of accolades. Pompey Magnus spent a significant portion of time restructuring the province, expanding his social network by building ties with the local elites there. It is sufficient to say that by the time he returned to Rome in 71 BC, he could count a number of the Spanish communities as his supporters. His return to Italy coincided with the conclusion of the Italian slave uprising led by Spartacus, known as the Third Servile War. The uprising began while the Romans were preoccupied with both the conflict in Spain, and the onset of the Third Mithridatic War of 74 BC. This was a time when Rome was bereft of legions at home, and the uprising threw the city into a state of crisis. The revolt rapidly gained momentum as Spartacus' successes drew thousands of slaves to his cause. It is estimated that the rebels numbered some 70,000 slaves, largely of Greek origin. Through the resourceful application of unconventional tactics, Spartacus successfully defeated a Roman army outside of Mount Garganus in 72 BC, which prompted the Roman senate to appoint Marcus Licinius Crassus to contend with the rebels. He was successful, defeating Spartacus' army. However, some remnants escaped from the battlefield and fled northwards. It was there that the surviving slaves ran into the returning legions led by Pompey Magnus, who promptly crushed the runaways. Nevertheless, both men equally claimed success for having brought the Spartacus revolt to a close, despite Crassus having done the lion's share of the fighting.

Ambition defined Pompey's life. There was no military venture that Rome undertook that he did not want to have some part in. Such was the case with the Third Mithridatic War — the last that Rome was to fight against Pontus. Mithradates the VI began the conflict by attempting to capitalize on Roman domestic turmoil. Lucius Licinius Lucullus and Marcus Aurelius Cotta had been charged with checking the Pontic King's advance, and securing the new Roman protectorate of Bythnia. Cotta, admiral of the Roman naval force in Asia, was checked by Mithradates, and left trapped behind the walls of the city of Chalcedon in Asia Minor. There, 64

Roman ships were captured, and the 3,000 Romans who manned them were slaughtered. Those who remained in Chalcedon could do nothing but wait for Lucullus' relief force. Mithridates did not tarry long in siege, and escaped to the city of Heraclea Pontica upon the Hellespont. The Roman armies pursued him to its gates. Cotta returned to Rome in 70 BC, leaving Lucullus in sole command of both Rome's Asiatic armies and overseeing the siege. Lucullus enjoyed a great degree of success, forcing Mithridates from Heraclea Pontica to Armenia where he was protected by the Armenian king, Tigranes the Great. Lucullus pursued his enemy, and defeated a large Armenian army that outnumbered the Romans almost two-to-one. He pressed his opponents, meeting Tigranes outside of the Armenian capital of Artaxia. There, the Armenian onslaught was tremendous. Lucullus' forces reeled by the charge of the Armenian cavalry, and were pushed against the banks of the Aratsani River. The Armenian heavy horse

crashed repeatedly against the Roman ranks —
rupturing their lines until Lucullus' men could
do no more but break ranks and flee. This was a
significant defeat for Rome.

Spying an opportunity to seize a new
command, Pompey coerced Lucullus' brother in
law, Publius Clodius Pulcher, into undermining
the authority of the Roman commander. This
Clodius did, until Lucullus' troops had mutinied
from his command. Disgraced, Lucullus was
forced to withdraw to Rome in 66 BC. He was
incensed at the prospect of having his command
removed. Successful, Pompey was given the
command of the Roman war efforts against
Mithridates and Tigranes.

Pompey's war effort in Asia was merciless. He
met Mithridates on the outskirts of the
Armenian kingdom and crushed him, forcing the
defeated Pontic king to retreat north to the
nation of Chalcis on the banks of the Black Sea.
Rather than pursue, Pompey then turned to
Armenia. He pillaged and plundered its

countryside as punishment for its treachery. Tigranes pleaded to Pompey for peace; a peace that was brokered only with the Armenian king becoming a client of Rome. Pompey then followed Mithridates up the Black Sea coastline through Chalcis and into Cimmeria. With the onset of winter, he was forced to return to Pontus. There, he was adamant that the former kingdom of Mithridates would become a new Roman province, and began appointing pro-Roman elites as Pontic officials. Mithridates continued through the Bosporus, arriving in Crimea at the citadel of Panticapaeum. There reigned his eldest son, Machares, who refused to help his father in his wars against Rome. Furious with his son's refusal, Mithridates had him murdered, and took control of his son's kingdom. However, Mithridates' youngest son, Pharnaces II, was disgusted with his father's conduct and his refusal to bring the war with Rome to an end. He raised an army in rebellion against his father, which ended with a near victory for Mithridates. Although victorious,

Mithridates was consumed with grief at the deaths of both of his sons. He first attempted suicide by poisoning, but his lifelong habit of taking minor doses of common poisons had rendered him immune. With nowhere else to turn, he asked his bodyguard to stab his heart in 64 BC.

So concluded the Third Mithridatic War, with Pompey being credited for the defeat and death of one of Rome's greatest rivals in the East. Pompey's victories were not constrained to the Pontic theatre, however. Stretching the scope of his military command, Pompey drove his forces into the remaining fragments of the Seleucid kingdom in Syria. There, he deposed its monarch, Antiochus XIII Asiaticus in 64 BC. This was an illegal act, undertaken without prior consent from the Senate. However, the senators benefited tremendously from his efforts. He reconstituted Syria as a Roman province, and then pushed further south towards the Pheonician lands of Coele-Syria. The plunder he amassed was significant. Spying internal weakness in Judea, Pompey then involved himself in its civil war, and supported Hyrcanus II against his rival Aristobulus II. Together, they surrounded the city of Jerusalem. Josephus, in his historical account of Roman involvement in Judea, writes that very few Romans fell compared to the "twelve thousand Jews" who perished in the sack. However, Pompey did not loot the city of its vast gold reserves and precious treasures in the Temple of Jerusalem. Instead, he appointed Hyrcanus' supporters to act as wards who were tasked with safeguarding their wellbeing. 62 BC came to a close with Pompey in total control of the Eastern Mediterranean. He had created four new provinces, Bythnia and Pontus, Syria, Cilicia, and Crete. Moreover, he had extended Roman dominion beyond the Black Sea and the Bosporus, and raised a number of client states that now acted on Rome's behalf. It was an impressive feat, a spree of conquests that earned him the utmost regard and jealousy at home in Rome. He was commemorated with a triumph in 61 BC: his 3rd one, at the young age of 45.

Marcus Licinius Crassus

Marcus Licinius Crassus was the second son of the eminent Roman senator, Publius Licinius Crassus, who had been consul in 97 BC, and censor in 89 BC. Due to his father and youngest brother's executions in the Marian War, Marcus Crassus was destined to be an enemy of Marius and Cinna. As a relative of a proscribed individual, Marcus was also added to the list of proscriptions. This forced him first to flee to Spain, and Africa after that. There he joined a band of Sulla's closest supporters who desperately awaited the exiled general's return. Following Sulla's return to Italy in 83 BC, Crassus openly declared himself in support of the future dictator alongside Metellus Pius. He was given command of the right wing during the battle of the Colline Gates, pushing his division through the Marian lines and encompassing the enemy — a decisive maneuver that would bring victory for Sulla. His success during this battle earned him tremendous praise from the dictator, and placed him among some of Sulla's most powerful followers.

From Plutarch's account, we know that the chief priority for Crassus following the civil war was to rebuild his family's fortune and regain their estates. These had been stolen from Crassus during Cinna's proscriptions of pro-Sulla elements in Rome. His method for achieving the return of his family's estate was typical of the time: the widespread proscription and execution of suspected Marians. He amassed a tremendous fortune by acquiring his enemy's property, which he then resold for a considerable return. Perhaps in an attempt to mar Crassus' reputation, Plutarch documented that Crassus had added to the list of those proscribed the names of men whose fortune he coveted. Whether there is any truth to these claims or not, it is likely that this was a common occurrence during the terrible days of proscription. Crassus was also known to employ an army of slaves acting as skilled firefighters and carpenters. With these resources at his disposal, he would opportunistically wait for fires and times of great public calamities. His method of operation was straightforward. The dense, compact nature of Rome made fires the most dangerous threats to public property, as blazes easily spread from one building to the next. During such an event, Crassus would arrive at the scene, and offer to purchase the endangered property from its owners for a pitiful sum. Should the owner accept his offer, he would then employ his seemingly endless supply of slaves to combat the blaze in an attempt to recover the property. If the owner refused Crassus' offer, the patrician would simply stand by and watch as the building burned to cinders. In his pursuit of wealth, Crassus was merciless and ever calculating, with many contemporary historians and biographers claiming his love of gold to exceed all other things. He frequently raised the rent on buildings under his possession, despite their obvious poor and deteriorating condition. He was atypical of Roman senators at the time, who were supposed to abstain from the wanton pursuit of wealth. Crassus had no care for such trappings. Pliny wrote that he was capable of taking two *sesterces* and transforming them into a thousand more.

Another financial source for Crassus was the lucrative commerce of slaves. He had tens of thousands of these due to robbing them from proscribed individuals. Moreover, Crassus had come to possess of a number of silver mines in Northern Italy and in Greece. These brought a considerable yearly return to his coffers, but paled in comparison to the income he had earned from the proscription.

With the consolidation of his fortunes, Crassus returned to the political realm with the intent of climbing the *cursus honorum*. Being a phenomenally wealthy supporter of Sulla, his political success was nearly a guarantee — were it not for the recent meteoric success of Pompey

Magnus. Magnus was then being heralded as Rome's new military hero for his successes fighting Marians throughout Sicily and North Africa. Already, Crassus was in danger of being eclipsed by the upstart, and still had to contend with other successful Roman generals like Licinius Lucullus and Metellus Pius. The outbreak of the Third Mithridatic War and the continued Spanish war against Sertorius presented opportunities for Crassus. However, he was overlooked in both instances. It was only the outbreak of the Third Servile War that presented Crassus with the opportunity to demonstrate his genius as a general. Even then, the Senate was reluctant to appoint him. It was following the Roman defeat at Mount Garganus in 72 BC that the Roman Senate was willing to give Crassus a chance, and only provided he supply and equip the legions at his own expense. It is apparent that the Senate clearly lacked confidence in Crassus' competence as a general. Moreover, they were disillusioned with the war against Spartacus as a whole — the slaves had beaten Roman armies on multiple occasions, and become a tremendous nuisance for peace in Italy. After a segment of his Roman army broke and fled after a skirmish with the slaves, Crassus reinstated the ancient practice of decimation. Decimation was the systematic execution of one individual out of ten from a legion that had fled in the face of the enemy. Its purpose was to raise the morale of the army and strengthen their resolution to fight. Appian makes it evident that the soldiers needed to fear Crassus more than Spartacus and his slaves.

The Third Servile War progressed in this manner, with Crassus pursuing Spartacus across the whole of Italy — eluding him at every turn, and continuing to raid and pillage the Italian countryside. To assist Crassus, the Senate recalled Pompey Magnus from his praetorship of Spain. Spartacus, upon discovering the Senate's plan, chose to engage Crassus' army rather than be trapped by Crassus and Pompey. What ensued was the Battle of the Siler River, a decisive victory for Crassus' legions. There they readily cut down the slaves, despite their terrain and numerical advantage. Spartacus was killed in that battle, and Crassus ordered that the entire surviving body of slaves who had not fled be crucified along the *Via Appia*. It was a gruesome sight: a scale of torture unprecedented in ancient history, and served as suiting testament to those who would revolt against Roman rule. Pompey arrived in Italy at a fortuitous time, mopping up whatever remnants of the slave revolt that had managed to escape from Crassus. For this, Pompey declared that he himself had won the victory over Spartacus, even though Crassus' actual victory was all the more spectacular. Pompey was attempting to steal from Crassus' glory, despite Plutarch remarking that the massacre of slaves was considered a dishonorable act, worthy of no fame. Despite this, Crassus received an ovation in the Senate house — an honor that was far below a triumph, but more than Plutarch believed he was entitled to. Crassus felt humiliated by this gesture, as he thought himself worthy of a triumph due to the amount of property and lives his actions had saved. He believed that the Senate's rebuff was a personal attack encouraged by Pompey, which only contributed to his animosity for the man. Such a reaction is understandable. Given Crassus' esteemed association with Sulla, and his vast possessions, Pompey would have considered him a dangerous rival and competitor as early as the Third Servile War. Moreover, although both men came from similar origins, they earned their wealth in vastly different ways. One earned his through military conquest, the other through opportunism and clever investments. Their ambition, and the hypercompetitive nature of elite politics in Rome, was pushing both men towards the brink of open hostility.

In recognition of the esteemed importance of both men, the Senate declared both Pompey and Crassus consuls in 70 BC. This was the same year as the return of the Roman general, Cotta, from the Asian front, and likely around the time that Pompey became aware of the lucrative opportunities offered by the Third Mithridatic War. Aware that his military exploits continued to pale in comparison to Pompey's, Crassus was resolved to have an impressionable year as consul. He displayed his exorbitant wealth in a magnificent banquet in honor of Hercules, and allowed the entire populace of Rome to gorge themselves at one of his ten thousand tables. It was a tremendous feast, and had cost him a substantial sum of money to host. To further impress the populace, Crassus also distributed a three-month supply of grain to each and every Roman family in the city. Such an act of generosity was singular in purpose, and typical of most aspiring Romans. By appearing to give back to his beloved city, Crassus was consolidating his own supremacy within the Senate. Despite these attempts at becoming Rome's greatest citizen, Crassus' hatred for Pompey would only continue to grow as the latter expanded Roman territories in Syria and the East in 65 BC. The fabulous wealth that resided in these eastern provinces must have drawn not only his ire, but also his curiosity as to the possibilities that lay therein. This source of wealth would provide a direction for Crassus' own future political motivation.

Chapter 3: The First Triumvirate

It is evident that as the middle of the century approached, political power and prestige were increasingly consolidated in the hands of two political juggernauts: Crassus and Pompey. There existed a mutual dislike between both men, and this created an extremely volatile situation in Rome as each man sought to undermine the other. However, unlike the political situation that defined the earlier civil war between Marius and Sulla, the Senate preserved its staunch opposition to both men. It is this hostility by the *optimates* that drove Crassus and Pompey to seek a partnership. Combined, they believed the Senate cease playing one man off of the other, and would be powerless to bar their legislation and sabotage their interests. Such an alliance was feasible, yet it lacked the means to prevent potential betrayals. What was necessary for its success was the entry of a third member. Such an opportunity presented itself in the form of a lesser, but equally ambitious senator by the name of Gaius Julius Caesar.

Gaius Julius Caesar

Gaius Julius Caesar belonged to the venerable clan, the *gens Julia*, which had been involved in the Roman Republic since its very foundation. His sect of the family was the *Julia Caesaris*, a minor branch of the family that had a more humble beginning when compared to the other sects of the family. The *Julia Caesaris'* emergence onto the political field began in the first century BC, when Caesar's father — also named Gaius Julius Caesar — attained the governorship of the province of Asia, after his aunt married Gaius Marius. What might have been a fortuitous marriage arrangement firmly entrenched the Caesars as Marians upon the outbreak of the Marius' war against Sulla. Caesar further strengthened this relationship to Marius through a marriage to Cinna's daughter. While politically advantageous in securing him the position of high priest of Jupiter, such an action earned him the ire of Sulla. The very same proscriptions that targeted so many of Sulla's enemies fell also on Caesar, who lost his dowry, property, official title and income. He was only saved from the grip of execution by entreaties on the part of his fellow *Julii*, who had been faithful supporters of Sulla.

Upon losing his office within the priesthood, Caesar was thrust into military life in an attempt to escape Sulla's potential retribution. He traveled abroad, serving Rome across the Mediterranean in places like Cilicia and Asia. It was a challenging life, but one that Caesar grew accustomed to. There, he developed many close ties with powerful princes and kings, and acquired the diplomatic skills that would later come to define his political career in Rome. With Sulla's death in 78 BC, he was encouraged to return home. However while en route to Rome, Caesar was abducted by pirates who held him hostage in exchange for ransom. Manacled to the prow of their ship, Caesar famously retained an air of superiority as he promised each of his captors that he would someday return to kill them all. The pirates laughed at his comments, setting him free once his ransom had been paid. Unfortunately for them, Caesar had said those words with the full intention of making good on his promise. He raised a fleet and cast off in pursuit of his former captors, catching and crucifying each one.

Caesar's climb through the curial offices began in full with his appointment as quaestor in 69 BC. As quaestor, he was tasked with supervising the financial expenses of the Roman Republic, and his duties included monitoring both its treasury and its expenditures on infrastructure and military campaigns. Through this appointment, Caesar earned the right to sit in the Senate, which exposed him to the political theatrics therein. He was remarkably cognizant of the social impetus towards extravagant spending, and knew that he needed to spend lavishly to earn a name for himself. In this endeavor, Caesar amassed a huge debt that numbered some eight million *sesterces*. He spent money with the greatest ease — purchasing property, slaves, and artworks. He even hosted some gladiator games. His arrogant spending habits earned him the ire of many senators, who believed him to be an impetuous "new man." Such expenses were necessary, however. As a former Marian, Caesar needed to establish his reputation. Furthermore, large expenses and purchases were already a required part of a senator's civic duty to the city. One rarely advanced up the curial ranks without spending a small fortune. Caesar's brief stint as a magistrate in the province of Spain sewed the seed of his terrible ambition — the same ambition that would come to fruition a decade later. There, he reflected on the great accomplishments of Alexander the Great, and rued his own petty victories in comparison.

What was necessary was the attainment of higher and better offices, which required that he secure more powerful friends. Such an opportunity presented itself with Pompey's bill of 66 BC. Being Rome's foremost general, Pompey desired the ability to act on the Senate's behalf and declare war autonomously throughout in Asia. This lack of Senatorial approval was vital for Pompey's conquests, which often depended on the timing of opportunistic attacks on weakened kingdoms, as exemplified by the Roman subjugation of Judea. By declaring his support for Pompey, Caesar established a connection to the man, which would only facilitate his later friendship. His subsequent appointment to the aedileship in 64 BC brought on new opportunities, but also new expenses. As aedile, Caesar was tasked with throwing lavish games and ceremonies on the State's behalf. A successful aedile was one who threw exorbitant parties that captured the attention and love of the people of Rome. However, such a position placed exorbitant stress on both the Senate's treasury, and his own financial resources. Such sacrifices were necessary, however. Next to the office of consul, the aedile was one of the most valued offices, as it offered a degree of public visibility that was simply incomparable. For someone like Caesar, this visibility was vital. It brought one to the political forefront and consolidated one's reputation. As a result of this appointment, Caesar descended further into debt, and his creditors began to worry that Caesar might not ever pay them back on their loans.

Caesar continued to climb the curial office, capitalizing on his opponents' weaknesses to ensure his own success. As a candidate for the position of supreme pontiff, Caesar highlighted the allegations of corruption and bribery that beset his opponents. Such a tactic easily secured him the office in 63 BC. This appointment bestowed tremendous prestige upon Caesar, granting him the religious and political authority that he so ardently desired. As pontiff, Caesar was tasked with the interpretation of divine acts, which offered him the advantage of attributing beneficial signs from the gods as being favorable to his friends.

It is readily apparent that Caesar's rise through the offices of the *cursus honorum* was rapid. This success had its drawbacks. His creditors increasingly demanded that their loans be repaid, even threatening to bring Caesar to trial before the courts. Such litigation could only be pursued once Caesar had relinquished his office, however. Faced with such demands that he simply could not satisfy, Caesar turned to yet another benefactor for aid: Marcus Licinius Crassus. Crassus was then the wealthiest man in Rome. Crassus at this time was keen to develop an alliance with Caesar, because he was ever mindful of the increasing popularity of his rival, Pompey Magnus. Crassus had secured Caesar's loyalty by offering to pay off a portion of his vast debt immediately, and acting as a guarantor for whatever remained of the sum. With Crassus' support, Caesar secured the praetorship of Spain. However, the threat of judicial action always loomed. It was imperative that Caesar avoided tarnishing the reputation that he had laboriously built. By becoming a propraetor, Caesar extended his service in office, which subsequently lengthened his period of judicial immunity. His governance in Spain is considered by many to have been excellent. There, he subjugated two hostile Lusitani and Arevaci tribes. Moreover, he extended the onus of Roman governance by restructuring the provincial lending laws to encourage Italian investment within Spain.

Come 60 BC, it was evident to all that Caesar was a remarkable political success. His rapid ascendancy of the *cursus honorum* had demonstrated this. However, it was an upward mobility facilitated by gold. In the process, he had made no shortage of enemies — particularly among those individuals who had loaned him considerable sums of money. Necessity had demanded that Caesar spend money that he simply did not possess. The only guarantee he could offer in return was the hope that he could obtain a military command in a wealthy province like Syria, which would have generated a great deal of income in the form of tribute and plunder. However, these very same loans that caused him so much trouble also brought him into discussion with the two leading men at the time: Pompey and Crassus. Then, each man was eager to enhance his own glory at the expense of the other. Their hatred for one another seemed irreconcilable. However, as the year approached, it became apparent that other factors within the Roman Senate were interested in curbing their successes. To overcome this adversity by the *optimates*, an alliance was necessary. Who better to bridge their differences than their mutual friend, Gaius Julius Caesar?

The Founding of the Triumvirate

The year 60 BC marked a time of considerable opposition demonstrated on the part of the Senate towards both Gnaeus Pompey Magnus and Marcus Licinius Crassus. Pompey, recently returned from Asia, was looking to consolidate Rome's victorious acquisitions in the region, and to also find lands upon which he could settle his veterans. Crassus sought to expand his interests in Syria, but also protect the *publicani* who had been operating in Asia Minor. The *publicani* — tax collectors who speculated on the value of tax returns for a given region — were then being barraged by legislation that sought to curb their influence on both local and senatorial politics. The *publicani* were considered Crassus' clients, and thus appealed to their patron in Rome. They wanted Crassus to invalidate the legislation and return them to their accustomed way of conducting business.

However, the Senate defeated each of these man's respective appeals, often by blatant dismissal on the part of either Crassus or

Pompey. Both men were exceedingly influential, and counted many senators among their supporters. It thus became rapidly evident that the Senate was becoming dichotomized between the two camps. Leading politicians like Cicero or Cato the Younger found themselves picking one side or another. Although both men had held a joint consulship, there existed no love between the two. Resolution between the two was necessary, and time was of the essence. Pompey's legions were becoming increasingly impatient and riotous with the Senate's refusal to found them a colony, and Pompey's image was suffering as a result. Moreover, Crassus own attempts at mediating on behalf of the *publicani* was failing, with no clear consensus among the senators as to the reasons for refuting the earlier legislation that had greatly restricted the tax collectors.

It was Julius Caesar who offered a solution to their predicament. He proposed an alliance between both men, which would in turn bring their own supporters into line with their interests. He reconciled this through diplomatic means, suggesting that each man wholeheartedly support the interests of the other, regardless of whatever consequences may arise. As a result, the majority of the Senate would vote in approval of any legislation that was to be passed by them. Such an overture was possible only due to Caesar's preexisting relationship with both men. Caesar already considered Crassus a patron due to the latter's grant of credit on his behalf. By creating an alliance, Caesar would be shifting the dynamic of their relationship towards one that more closely reflected an equal partnership. Pompey proved more difficult to win over to Caesar's cause. Although Caesar had supported Pompey's bill regarding the grant of emergency powers in 66 BC, their relationship was only cordial. To both win Pompey's trust and consolidate his relationship with him, Caesar offered his daughter Julia's hand in marriage. Caesar knew that Pompey was infatuated with Julia, and considered the joining of the families to be of great political advantage. Although Julia was thirty years younger than Pompey, she too found herself in love with the man, and was a virtuous and devoted wife to her husband. Although politically motivated, the marriage made Pompey and Caesar the dearest of friends.

Each man benefited tremendously from the alliance, but he with the most to gain was Caesar. By creating the Triumvirate, Caesar had drawn a close relationship to the two most powerful men in the city. In the span of his years, Caesar had taken his family's reputation from relative obscurity, and thrust it among Rome's most famous names.

Although the alliance had been made, the Triumvirate was to remain a secret. The reasoning for this was to avoid prematurely arousing any suspicion amongst their opponents within the Senate — Marcus Tullius Cicero being of principal concern. Cicero, a fellow new man, was a famous orator and advocate. He had recently enjoyed tremendous success for bringing the Second Catilinarian Conspiracy of 63 BC to an end. The Second Catilinarian Conspiracy was a plot to slaughter the leading members of both the plebeian and patrician orders. If successful, it would have resulted in the murder of the majority of the Senate, and established in its stead a small, patrician-led oligarchy. As acting consul, Cicero's means for bringing the conspiracy to a conclusion was through the execution of all conspirators without trial. Cicero understood that such a decision was an illegal act, yet knew that expediency was necessary in bringing the conspiracy to a swift resolution. Far better an easy resolution than the inevitable quagmire of a Senatorial decision. Himself an ally of Pompey, Cicero was wary of the ambition of Caesar and the greed of Crassus.

Despite this opposition, the Triumvirate succeeded in achieving its first goal, which was the appointment of Caesar as consul. Through the support of Caesar and Crassus, Caesar acquired the consulship of 59 BC, alongside the conservative Marcus Bibulus. It was then that the alliance of the Triumvirate was first unveiled. Caesar sought to instigate his agrarian legislation of 59 BC before the Assembly of the People. Being populist in nature, the law drew tremendous opposition from the *optimates*. The legislation sought to redistribute lands in Italy to the poorest denizens of Rome, and enjoyed tremendous support from the Roman public. However, Caesar's law was highly divisive, and was so opposed that even his co-consul Bibulus sought to prevent its approval. However, to the surprise of the Senate, both Crassus and Pompey declared their endorsement of it, with Pompey even going so far as having flooded the streets of Rome with his legionaries. The potential for open hostilities when combined with the unanimous support of the fellow triumvirs passed the law within the Assembly of the People. Despite its success in the Senate, Bibulus remained ardently opposed to it, and decreed that he had witnessed such religious acts that demonstrated a strong divine disfavor with the agrarian law. In response, supporters of Caesar attacked Bibulus and his bodyguards. The riotous mob broke Bibulus' ceremonial *fasces*, and confined him to his home for the duration of his consulship. The consulship of 59 BC thereby became entirely Caesar's. As consul, Caesar fulfilled his promises to each of his fellow triumvirs. For Pompey, he established both a veteran's colony and legitimized his conquests in Asia. For Crassus, he alleviated the punitive legislation that harangued the *publicani*.

It soon became apparent to the Senate that the city was in the grip of a small oligarchy. Roman laws and interests were now being dictated by an alliance of its three most distinguished men. Although Pompey and Crassus were largely untouchable — being protected by wealth and a vast clientele— the Senate could still curtail Caesar's influence. In an effort to humiliate the consul, the Senate decreed that his consulship was to be held in the fields and the woods rather than a province. Attacking the weakest member of the Triumvirate had the potential of weakening the entire faction, and could have brought Pompey and Crassus once more into open opposition. However, the Senate underestimated the strength of their alliance. Angered by such a brazen attack on his office, Caesar turned once more to his political allies, who secured for him the governance of the Roman province of Cisalpine Gaul and Illyria. The Roman frontier of Transalpine Gaul (modern-day France) was later added, combined with the grant of four legions. With this army, Caesar was to protect the Roman dominion from any potential incursions. Perhaps to shield Caesar from future judicial action, Pompey, Crassus and their supporters all decreed that his governance of Rome's Gallic territories was to last for five years, rather than the traditional one year. This protected Caesar from whatever charge the Senate might be able to trump against him. Lastly, with the guarantee of legions in addition to the promise of a five-year office, the stage was set for Caesar's greatest success: his conquest of Gaul.

To rid themselves of any potential obstacles to their rule, the Triumvirate set about attacking their enemies by targeting them for exile. One of these was Marcus Tullius Cicero. To undermine Cicero's authority, the Triumvirate employed one of their tools: Publius Clodius Pulcher. Previously Pompey's friend, Clodius was now a populist senator. He belonged to the patrician *gens Claudia*, an illustrious clan dating back to the founding of the Roman state. A calculating and innovative legislator, Clodius had the misfortune of involving himself in a number of scandals over the course of his political career. He was a demagogue who drew hostility and bred rumor. The first scandal in which he was involved was during his service under Lucullus in Rome's Asiatic armies. It was rumored then that he had fraternized with the general's wife, which prompted Lucullus to divorce her. The second scandal occurred during the Second

Catilinarian Conspiracy. Cicero targeted Clodius as a conspirator, despite his blatant innocence. Clodius was incensed with Cicero, as the advocate was his brother-in-law. By trying to charge Clodius, Cicero was likely trying to revenge himself on the *gens Claudia* for their meddling in his marital affairs. Previously, Clodius' sister had attempted to convince Cicero to divorce his wife, Terentia, and marry her instead.

The most jarring of Clodius' scandals occurred during the festival of Bona Dea in Rome. This was during Caesar's term in office as supreme pontiff in 63 BC. The festival of Bona Dea was a celebration for Roman women only. As a result, men were forbidden from entering the sacred premises under penalty of death. As Caesar was supreme pontiff, it was natural that the religious processions would be held within his home for the duration of the festival. Clodius was then in an extramarital affair with Caesar's wife Pompeia, and had been caught while attempting to infiltrate Bona Dea while disguised as a woman. Ashamed, Caesar promptly divorced his wife. However, he surprisingly refused to charge Clodius with the necessary punishment. Instead, he gave Clodius the benefit of the doubt — despite the latter's reputation for womanizing. By pretending to know nothing of the affair and agreeing with Clodius' alibi, Caesar protected the guilty man from capital punishment: an act that would place Clodius in Caesar's debt. Regardless of the truth of the accusations, Cicero, as litigator tasked with overseeing the trial, was determined to bring Clodius to account for his crimes. However, he was powerless before the actions of the Triumvirate. Plutarch documents how Crassus had successfully secured the acquittal of Clodius by bribing the jurors. Aware that these acts were not done altruistically, Clodius became a loyal client of both Caesar and Crassus, aligning himself in support of their political interests.

Perhaps most striking about Clodius' bizarre political career is his adoption into the plebeian *gens Fonteii* in 59 BC. In doing so, Clodius forsook his paternal tie to the patrician caste for that of the plebeians. It is likely that this was at the behest of Caesar's wishes. It was an act that stood in direct contradiction with the principles underlying Roman adoption law. Despite this, the adoption was approved, even though Fonteius was far younger than Clodius. By becoming a plebeian elite, Clodius became a candidate for the position of Tribune of the Plebs, and successfully acquired the office early in Caesar's consulship.

Opposition towards Cicero defined Clodius' term as Tribune. Early in his term, Clodius passed a law that forbade the execution of any Roman citizen without a fair trial. Such a law intentionally targeted Cicero, who had previously executed the conspirators in the Catilinarian Conspiracy without trial. This had been a necessary but fatal flaw on Cicero's part.

Although he had ended the conspiracy, he had committed a gross error that violated Roman law. Many senators were willing to forgive Cicero for his use of emergency actions, but not Clodius. Through Clodius incessant haranguing, Cicero was exiled from Rome. His greatest enemy removed as an obstacle, Clodius' attacks against Cicero grew all the more brazen. Clodius decreed that Cicero was forbidden from entering within 400 miles of the Italian peninsula, and seized all of his property on the Italian mainland. Cicero was thus deprived of his property, with much of it being burned down by angry mobs. To inflame the passions of the people, and bring them to his cause, Clodius enacted his *leges Claudii*, which granted a free grain dole to every citizen in Rome. Clodius further reduced the Senate to a farce by decreeing it illegal to declare certain omens on certain days. This was done to prevent any of his opponents from dismissing his laws under religious pretexts. Clodius also passed a law that forbade the censors from barring any citizen from accessing the Senate. Aware of the increasing role of violence in Roman politics, Clodius created a number of clubs and guilds known as *collegia*. Far from being a guild, these gangs were in reality a group of thugs that operated on his behalf. These gangs roamed the streets of Rome, and intimidated the populace at Clodius' behest.

Thus, Clodius strengthened his hold on Rome, but he was ever mindful of his subservience to the Triumvirate. He was loyal, and knew his place. Operating on their behalf, he annexed the kingdom of Cyprus to the Roman Empire, and charged Cato with a praetorian command over the island. This was done to remove Cato from the city of Rome, as he had begun to demonstrate a certain dislike and resistance towards the Triumvirate.

Thus we have seen that through strength of force and the exile of its enemies, the Triumvirate had thrust itself to the political forefront in Rome and seized control. This alliance of Caesar, Crassus, and Pompey was something new altogether: a shared system of oligarchy that was founded on the mutual agreement to not intervene in one another's interests. With Caesar acting as intermediary, the Triumvirate successfully instigated its plans and secured its objectives. For Caesar, these were the consulship and the passing of his agrarian law. For Pompey, it was land for his veterans, and the grant of legality over his conquests in Asia. Crassus desired that his Asian financial interests and those of his clients be protected in the wake of Senatorial intervention. Their methods of achieving this were innovative.

Through the appointment of Publius Clodius Pulcher as Tribune of the Plebs, the Triumvirate was capable of protecting its legislation from being overturned in following years. Clodius was their man. He acted on their behalf, and protected their interests. Through his gangs, he effectively disarmed the Senate on behalf of the Triumvirate. As Caesar departed for his command in Gaul, it seemed as if political affairs in Rome were beginning to stabilize at last.

Chapter 4: Caesar in Gaul

Julius Caesar's departure for Cisalpine Gaul in 58 BC marked an important juncture for the trajectory of Roman military expansion. Prior conquests had intended to subjugate the known world, areas with a long history of urbanization: places like Carthage, Greece, and Asia. These areas were known for their wealth and affluence, and therefore proved a profitable target for military operations. Come 58 BC, however, such nations were already subjugated. Carthage and the Hellenistic kingdoms fell in the Second Century; Mithridates and Pontus in the first, and the Iberian tribes of Spain were slowly being introduced into the Roman state by Pompey's earlier efforts at provincial establishment. Truly, only the Ptolemaic kingdom of Egypt remained, and it was long subservient to Rome's interests as a client-kingdom. Therefore, for an ambitious general seeking to establish a reputation for military glory, new ground needed to be broken.

Gaul: A History

Historically, the region beyond the Alps known as Gaul had long mystified the Roman consciousness. Its inextricable connection to the Italian peninsula loomed ominous in many Roman minds, and the populace often feared Gallic incursions. This was due to the scars earned from previous invasions on the part of Gallic tribes. The first major invasion came from the Senones, who had established themselves in northern Italy during the days of the early Republic. A Roman effort to dislodge the newcomers at Allia — on the confluence of the rivers of the Tiber— had failed, leaving the city vulnerable to sack by the Senones. The city of Rome lay bare to the Celtic (Another term for Gallic) horde, and was stripped of its defenders. It was brutally sacked in 390 BC, with many Romans cut down in the streets while trying to defend their homes. Some of the city's inhabitants had clustered and taken shelter within the Roman fortress atop the Capitoline hill, and therefore survived the pillaging. Such an event had a tremendous effect on the Roman mentality towards Celts, and they came to regard the population as one of their most despised enemies.

Gallic involvement in Roman affairs continued. The Second Punic War fought against the Carthaginians brought Rome into newfound conflict with the Gallic tribes beyond the Alps. The Carthaginian general, Hannibal, had aspired to win over a number of allies in Italy. To accomplish this, he sent his agents to Italian cities to create dissatisfaction with Roman rule. Easily won over to his side were the Celtic inhabitants of Cisalpine Gaul, who had only recently been subjugated by the Romans as a result of the Gallic War of 225 BC. Hannibal's presence in Italy caused a general uprising among the tribes of the Boii and Insubres, who halted the Roman colonization at Placentia and Cremona. The ranks of the Carthaginian army — greatly depleted due to attrition from their crossing of the Alps — were replenished by these new additions. Celtic warriors fought for Hannibal in a number of battles, serving at the Roman massacre on the River Trebia in 217 BC. They were involved in the subsequent slaughter at Lake Trasimene in the following year, which saw yet another Roman army defeated in Italy. Their pivotal role was played at the Battle of Cannae in 216 BC. Hannibal used his Celtic auxiliaries to compose the center of his army, spreading his Libyan and Carthaginian troops on the wings. At the center, the Celts had the important task of keeping the two Roman armies contested while Hannibal's wings enveloped their enemy. This they did, with the striking success that made Cannae such a remarkable victory for the Carthaginians. Cannae was the most terrible defeat suffered by Republican Rome, with 80,000 of their soldiers perishing there.

It is therefore apparent that the Gallic tribes and the Romans had a certain historical animosity between them. This continued in the Late Republic, with the Germanic invasions of the Cimbri and Teutones in 113 BC being so fresh in the minds of the populace. There existed a fear of Gauls, whether they fell on the near or far side of the Alps. This, and the fact that most Gallic tribes inhabited rural villages rather than urban settlements, made them a poor choice for military conquest, as the promise of plunder was not readily apparent to Roman commanders.

Gaul in the First Century BC

Gaul in the mid-first century BC presented a tremendous opportunity for Caesar. Caesar, ever the pragmatist, was aware of the difficulties inherent in undergoing an Eastern conquest, despite it long being considered as the preference for Roman commands. It was widely known to be a wealthy region, which made it highly desired by Roman senators. Moreover, the

East fell already under the influence of the Parthians, who were successors of the ancient Persian Empire. Any Roman incursion there was bound to draw the Republic into conflict with this juggernaut, which would have lasted beyond the scope of a typical consular term in office. In being appointed Cisalpine Gaul and Illyria, Caesar successfully avoided raising suspicion on the part of the Senate. At the time, the province remained sparsely populated, having only just begun to urbanize as a result of Roman influence. It is likely that the Senate believed this to be a favorable appointment: Caesar receiving an extraordinary command in Cisalpine Gaul was unlikely to have any serious ramifications for the Roman state — even if he was to hold it for five years. Moreover, it removed Caesar from Rome itself, which facilitated the possibility for the *optimates* to undermine some of the changes created by the Triumvirate. In Cisalpine Gaul, Caesar could have his command over the woods and the wilderness.

Caesar's intentions become discernable when we consider why his political allies had secured him four legions and the addition of Transalpine Gaul to his command. In acquiring such resources, the Triumvirate had effectively created the possibility for Caesar to commence the military campaign that he desired. What was necessary was that this campaign appeared defensive and in protection of Rome's interests. Were it not to be, Caesar's command would be rescinded, and he would be sent home to await judicial trial for his debts. To maintain such appearances, Caesar had to calculate a course of action that would align with Rome's concept of *jus bellum* — just war. *Jus bellum* is the term given to Rome's policy of fighting a justified war. It implies that Rome or one of its allies was attacked, and that the military action undertaken by the Republic was in defense of its territory or its values. Idealistic, and far from the reality of Roman expansion, *jus bellum* granted Rome the moral underpinnings that warranted its conquests to the Senate. It was necessary for

Caesar to operate within such a framework. He gathered intelligence on the movements of the Gallic tribes that lay just beyond the boundaries of Transalpine Gaul, and waited for the opportune moment to strike.

The opportunity presented itself in 58 BC, when the Helvetii — a confederacy of Gallic tribes residing within the Swiss plateau — undertook a mass migration, searching for new lands to establish themselves. Historically, such mass movements were always disruptive, greatly stressing local resources as a tribe moved from place to place. However, the Helvetii were resolved that their passing be a peaceful one. They sent out numerous embassies to nearby tribes to guarantee their safe passage. These secured, the Helvetii burned their former villages so as to discourage any elements within the confederacy from considering abandoning the migration. Their charted course would have taken them westward from the Swiss plateau, and moved them through the lands of both the

Aedui and Transalpine Gaul. Caesar learned of their migration while governing in Cisalpine Gaul, and hastily crossed the Alps with one legion to rescue his threatened province. Determined to check their advance, Caesar ordered the destruction of the Rhone Bridge and raised auxiliaries in Geneva to bolster his forces. The Helvetii sent an embassy to negotiate their peaceful transit through the Roman dominion. Caesar was resolved not to let the tribe pass, being aware of the former destruction wrought by the Cimbri and Teutones upon the Italian peninsula half a century earlier. Instead, Caesar stalled the negotiations for fifteen days while he fortified his position. The fifteen days having elapsed, the Helvetii returned, but only to be refused by Caesar. Indignant at such a rebuke, elements within the Helvetii attempted a series of attacks on the Roman fortifications, but were easily beaten back. Halted at the entrance of Transalpine Gaul, they opted instead to reach their destination by detouring through the lands of the Sequani. Along the way, they pillaged the

Aedui, who were a Roman ally. Having both attacked a Roman magistrate and their ally; Caesar had been given the pretext for war that he so ardently desired. He hastened back to Cisalpine Gaul and retrieved his three other legions, while raising a fourth in the process. Together with the legion already stationed in Transalpine Gaul, Caesar launched himself past the Roman frontier and led his five legions in pursuit of the Helvetii, who then were wreaking a trail of destruction across the lands of the Aedui, Ambarri and Allobroges. These tribes each appealed to Caesar for help, as they were incapable of opposing the gargantuan Helvetii. Caesar obliged them, and caught the Helvetii by surprise as they were crossing the Arar River. The crossing was largely complete, however — save for one Helvetii tribe known as the Tigurini. The Tigurini remained trapped on one bank of the river, and awaited the arrival of boats to bring them across. Isolated from the rest of the band, the Tigurini were hastily defeated by Caesar's legions, who drove their people into the depths of the river's rapids. He pursued the remaining Helvetii across the Arar River, and sent a force of 4000 legionaries supplemented with a small cohort of auxiliary Gallic cavalry ahead. A small cohort of Helvetian cavalry ambushed this force. In the ensuing skirmish, a general rout took place among the auxiliaries, which forced Caesar's troops to return to the larger army. This setback shook Caesar's confidence, and he retreated towards the Aedui town of Bibracte in central Gaul with the Helvetii in pursuit. The ensuing Battle of Bibracte is described in Caesar's *Gallic Wars* as being one of the most fiercely fought battles of his campaign, upon which the future of the Roman expedition in Gaul depended. The Romans and their Aedui allies fought the Helvetii for the majority of the day. Exhausted by the incessant fighting, the Helvetii conceded victory after Caesar succeeded in overturning their flank. Caesar accepted the Helvetian surrender, and ordered that they return to their homeland. His intent was to use the Helvetii as a buffer zone between the Roman frontier and the fierce Gallic and Germanic tribes that lay to their north.

Following his success over the Helvetii, Caesar was approached by the leading men among the Aedui regarding a looming Germanic threat that had established itself in the lands of the Sequani. Ariovistus, a German king, ruled the tribe that was known as the Suebi. The territory the Suebi occupied had been given to them as a reward for their assistance of the Sequani in a war against the Aedui. It is evident then that the Aedui had a tangible grievance with Ariovistus, and sought to capitalize on Caesar's involvement in Gallic territorial disputes to regain their lost lands. This suited Caesar's purposes well. A war with Ariovistus would strengthen the loyalty of Caesar's legions, and offer him a new opportunity to further expand Rome's dominions to the banks of the Rhine. Moreover, Caesar would be acting on behalf of a Roman ally, the Aedui. The only difficulty lay in overcoming Ariovistus' status as a friend of the

Roman people, which had been bestowed upon him by a Senatorial decree in 59 BC. Any declaration of war against Ariovistus would require a strong justification. Learning of one, Caesar declared that Ariovistus was to return the hostages he had taken years before from the Aedui. Moreover, he stated that no more Germanic tribes were to migrate across the Rhine river. He avowed that any violation of these stipulations was to be perceived as an act of war against Rome. In response, Ariovistus stated that both he and Caesar were conquerors, and that neither had the right to dictate how the other managed their affairs. Also, Ariovistus could not promise the halt of future migrations of Germanic tribes, as their movements were beyond his power to control.

The catalyst for the looming conflict lay in the discovery of a mass migration of countless Suebian tribes, who each intended to across the Rhine at some point within the year. For Caesar's province, this represented an exceptionally tangible threat. Such a movement of people would be difficult for the Roman governor to contain, as its size far eclipsed the forces he held at his disposal. What was necessary was a swift and decisive victory over Ariovistus. Ariovistus had then been preoccupied with his war against both the Aedui and his former allies, the Sequani. He had set his sights on the Sequani city of Vesontio. Apprising this, Caesar began marching his army towards the city, however the terrible legacy of Ariovistus and his hordes struck terror into the hearts of many of his soldiers. To instill his men with courage, Caesar humiliated them, declaring that the only legion he could trust was his favored tenth legion, and that he would go to war with this army alone. Disgraced, the subsequent legions could follow Caesar or else face the sting of shame for having abandoned their general.

Hesitant to engage an army of Rome, Ariovistus expressed his desire to speak to Caesar. The two met on the plains before the city of Vesontio. However, the meeting was cut short when a small force of Germanic horsemen encroached upon the negotiations and hurled projectiles at the Romans. Caesar and his bodyguard broke from the meeting and returned to the Roman camp. Ariovistus asked for a second meeting, but Caesar feared potential treachery. Instead, he sent two legates to negotiate on his behalf. Humiliated that Caesar would not dignify him with his presence, Ariovistus had both ambassadors thrown into chains. This gave Caesar the impetus he needed to strike at Ariovistus. Resolute in his decision to make battle, Caesar began planning on how best to bait the Germanic host into combat. A few inconclusive skirmishes occurred, offering no great advantage to either side. Ever wary of the looming tribal hordes that lay just beyond the Rhine, Caesar pressed for battle, lining up his army one morning and marching directly for the Suebian camp. Ariovistus hastily prepared his seven tribes, which had not adequately rested the night before. What ensued was a difficult battle for Caesar — tasked as he was with defeating a Germanic army that outnumbered him by several thousand. Due to its sheer size, the Suebi began pushing back the Roman left flank, which prompted Caesar to give the order for relieving forces to reinforce it. Moreover, he ordered Publius Crassus — son of Marcus Crassus — to charge the flank with the auxiliary cavalry. It was a defining point in the battle. Crassus' cavalry swept the Germanic force from behind, and sewed confusion among the German ranks. The addition of fresh Roman forces to the beleaguered left further frightened the Suebi, who began to rout in the face of what seemed like an overpowering show of force. Fear spread rapidly through the entire Suebi battle line, resulting in a general break. Caesar ordered that the Germans were to be pursued and cut down, which resulted in over a hundred thousand Suebi being killed or enslaved. Ariovistus, however, was not among them. He had managed to escape back across the Rhine, never to be seen in Gaul again.

The year 57 BC saw the sparks of another conflict in Gaul, which was eagerly undertaken by Caesar. A confederation of Belgian tribes had begun attacking Caesar's allies to the north. Pleased with his victory over Ariovistus, Caesar marched to meet them. However, among them were the Nervii, the fiercest and most cunning warriors in Gaul. They laid in ambush for Caesar, striking his army when it was setting camp for the night. What resulted was the Battle of the Sabis, where the Belgae advanced so rapidly that Caesar was incapable of organizing his legions into battle lines. Their onslaught was so fierce that it nearly resulted in a decisive defeat for Caesar. In the chaos, the majority of Caesar's officers and centurions were slain. Despite the ferocity of their attack, Caesar's tenth legion stood its ground, and allowed the scattered army a point around which to rally. Capable of finally redeploying, the Roman army thrust back the Belgian host, causing a number of its confederate tribes to break and flee from the conflict. However, the Nervii themselves stood fast, and refused to cower from the hail of missiles that Caesar's archers and slingers cast in their direction. Instead, they locked their shields together and awaited each successive barrage until the mounds of the fallen formed ramparts atop which they could fight. Caesar then employed his field artillery — ballistae and scorpions — to great effect. Gradually, all of the Nervii were slain, as none were seen to have fled. Such a show of bravery thoroughly impressed Caesar. Although defeated, the Belgae remained unbroken. Only the threat of the complete annihilation of their villages pushed them to offer a surrender, which Caesar magnanimously accepted. Victorious once more, Caesar brought Belgium into the Roman fold.

Caesar turned to the Atlantic coast. There resided the Veneti, who despised Rome's encroachment into Gaul and formed an anti-Roman confederation to resist their advance. This confederation was defensive in nature, yet Caesar cleverly manipulated the fact that they took nearby allies as hostages as a pretext for war. As the Veneti were a seafaring people, it was necessary that Caesar destroy their naval capacity in order to effectively disarm and pacify them. Construction of an Atlantic fleet occupied a prolonged period of time, in which Caesar was compelled to wait until the year 56 BC to begin his offensive. Caesar's initiative was somewhat of an experiment, in that the Romans had never before attempted naval combat upon the Atlantic Ocean. Their triremes, moreover, proved ill suited to combating the sailed vessels of the Veneti. The latter skirted the triremes with superior speed and maneuverability, firing arrows and hurling spears broadside. However, a fortuitous change in weather brought a lull in the winds, bringing the Veneti boats to a halt. This allowed the Roman triremes to use their oars to catch their enemies, which brought Caesar a decisive victory. The Veneti surrendered to Caesar and agreed to supply him with naval vessels and seamen.

Perhaps to commemorate his victory or remind the Suebi of their defeat at his hand, Caesar constructed a bridge across the Rhine and marched in a triumphal procession into Germania in 55 BC. Intended as a show of Roman superiority, Caesar was prepared to embark on a punitive expedition against his former enemies. However, across the Rhine, Caesar heard chilling rumors of the reason for the earlier Suebian migrations. Its catalyst was a far greater horde, which roamed just beyond the vast forests of Germania in the Scythian plains. It had attacked the Suebi, causing them to flee in droves towards Gaul. Some posit that Caesar's decision to return across the Rhine was to avoid provoking such a horde into conflict. To ward off the possibility of a future invasion, Caesar dismantled the bridge across the Rhine. Regardless of whether or not the bridge remained intact, he had sufficiently established himself as the first Roman to ever lead an army across the Rhine.

Caesar had firmly established a reputation for himself in Gaul and in Rome. His vanquishing of numerous Gallic kings and tribes demonstrated that he was a skilled leader of men, and a bringer of great victories to the Roman state. He was not satisfied with these victories. He wanted to further expand upon his legacy. Such ambition is unsurprising when we consider the previous comparison of himself with Alexander the Great. Caesar turned his attention northwards, across the English Channel and towards the mysterious island known as Britain. It was home of relatives of the Gauls known as Britons. With two legions, Caesar embarked on an expedition to the island, setting eyes on it for the first time in the latter half of that year. The Roman landfall was met by disaster: bad weather having wrecked a number of their vessels, which left them stranded in a little known part of the world. Moreover, they were soon met by a British show of force, whose warriors had descended upon the beaches riding chariots. Such an unfamiliar sight shook the nerves and spread fear among the Roman expedition. Many of the British were entirely naked — save for the blue war paint that adorned their bodies. These warriors screamed and yelled at the Romans from a distance, although they did not engage in combat with them. Eventually, the weather abated and the repairs of the Roman triremes were completed, which allowed for their safe return to the European mainland. However, Caesar was not content with having just made landfall in Britain. He became resolved to conquer a portion of the island. He returned in 54 BC, having brought a far more substantial army. Upon the river Thames, he met the Cattuvelauni, led by their king Cassivellaunus and engaged the tribe in battle. A ferocious struggle was undertaken, with the British chariots plunging themselves deep into Roman ranks. Despite the alien nature of the land and its people, the Romans emerged victorious from the battle, and forced the Cattuvelauni to pay tribute to the Roman state. Such gestures were wholly symbolic. Caesar had little intention to establish a permanent Roman presence in Britain. What he desired was the influence and prestige that the conquest in Britain afforded him. No other Roman senator could equally say that they too had led an expedition to the mysterious island of Britain and subjugated one of its peoples.

Following his victory over Cassivellaunus, Caesar returned to Gaul to find the Roman holdings there in disarray. Discontent had spread through the subjugated Gauls, leading many of their kings to enter into a secret alliance against Caesar. The winter of 54 BC marked the onset of their rebellion, led by the Eburones under Ambiorix. The northeastern Gallic confederations joined their cause, striking at the Romans wintering at Atuatuca Tungrorum in Belgium. There, the fourteenth legion, led by Quintus Titurius Sabinus, was taken by surprise and destroyed by the rebellious Gauls. A similar situation was narrowly avoided in a nearby Roman camp by the quick thinking of Quintus Tullius Cicero, brother to the esteemed Marcus

Tullius Cicero. Quintus had miraculously learned of the Gaul's looming betrayal, and thus sealed the camp's gates shut. There, his garrison repelled a myriad of attacks throughout much of the winter, surviving until Caesar could arrive and relieve his beleaguered soldiers. The following year was dedicated to a series of punitive expeditions undertaken against the Eburones, who were annihilated for their opportunistic transgressions against Caesar's armies and their slaughter of the soldiers at Atuatuca Tungrorum. Caesar then wielded his formidable panoply of an army to quickly vanquish the rebellion that had fomented amidst the Veneti. Caesar's victory delivered a crushing blow against Gallic independence. However, it succeeded only in further alienating the subjugated peoples of Gaul against the Roman state.

The vanquished confederacies turned now to the Arverni leader Vercingetorix, who had begun a series of revolts against the Roman efforts in Gaul. Vercingetorix cut a striking figure. He was the son of Celtillus, who had been a nobleman that aspired to rule over all of Gaul. Celtillus' wishes had been cut short, however, by a betrayal on the part of his own people. His son had inherited his ambition. Leading the poor and the downtrodden, Vercingetorix succeeded in overthrowing his opponents within the Arverni nobility and established himself as their king. Having secured his title, he undertook the next step of his rebellion. Previous revolts, such as that led by Ambiorix and the Eburones had failed because they enjoyed only local support. Vercingetorix knew that the only hope the Gallic peoples had of winning was through unification of all Gauls under a common alliance. He had tremendous appeal to his fellow downtrodden Gauls, which he employed to unite the disparate Gallic tribes in a common front against Caesar. Vercingetorix was aware of the dangers of engaging Roman armies in open battle, which was demonstrated to be a futile practice. The previous defeats suffered by individual Gallic tribes had emphasized this truth. Instead he decided to pursue a strategy of scorched earth, in which the Gallic communities would destroy their own villages and farms to deny the Romans the convenience of their use. This was intended to choke Caesar's lines of supply by curtailing the resources available to him, which would have placed tremendous pressure on his campaign. Vercingetorix was aware of Caesar's cleverness as a tactician. What was necessary was an innovation of the traditional Gallic battle formations. He introduced contemporary military tactics — shield and spear walls, javelins, and other projectiles — with the intent of competing with the rigid formations and excellent discipline of the Roman legionaries.

52 BC marked the beginning of Vercingetorix's campaign against Caesar, where he sought to profit from Caesar's preoccupation in Cisalpine Gaul and the ensuing turmoil in Rome. His allies, the Carnutes, made the first move against Rome: slaughtering the colonists

who had begun to settle the city of Cenabum. This outbreak was followed by the widespread slaughter of Roman settlers and merchants in every Gallic city. Having discovered this rebellion, Caesar mobilized his army and began to move across the Alps. It was then that Vercingetorix's plan was set in motion: he began razing every holding along Caesar's march from the south. His people, long accustomed to life in Gaul, would be capable of subsisting off of the land. The Romans, however, had to rely upon the importation of grain for their sustenance — a weakness that Vercingetorix sought to exploit. His burnings stretched wide and far. Caesar arrived in Gaul to find that the landscape had entirely changed in his absence. Where previously he had obtained supplies or shelter, he discovered only ash. To contend with the rebels, he split his army in half. The six legions under the command of Titus Labienus were sent to the north to contend with the Senones and Parisii tribes. Caesar himself was to contend with Vercingetorix and his Arverni.

The only city to have escaped
Vercingetorix's destruction was that of
Avaricum, the capital of the Biturges. The
inhabitants had pleaded with Vercingetorix to
spare them the fires. To this request he
reluctantly consented, but decreed that he would
not assist in their defense should Caesar attack.
Abandoning them to their fate, Vercingetorix
watched from afar as the hungry and exhausted
Roman legions besieged Avaricum. For days,
they surrounded the city, constructing
earthworks and siege machines. Mad with
hunger, Caesar's legions attacked on the 25th day
of the siege, and poured over Avaricum's walls to
slaughter the inhabitants of the city in anger for
their resistance. Of the 35,000 inhabitants, only
800 were spared. Avaricum was a fortuitous
victory for Caesar, as it possessed substantial
stores of grain and offered him the opportunity
to finally resupply his armies. The slaughter of
its inhabitants was a regrettable, albeit necessary
course of action. It instilled his soldiers with

morale and allowed them to ease their growing frustration of the elusive enemy.

Vercingetorix' hosts continued to elude Caesar, leading him further into the Gallic heartland. He had hoped to sufficiently tire the Roman army, so as to facilitate the inevitable battle. Caesar was aware of his opponent's strategy, and became increasingly resolved to risk a lack of supplies in order to bring the Arverni army into open combat. He marched on Gergovia, Vercingetorix' home. Gergovia was an Arverni city founded atop a plateau, which made it a highly defensible position. Within it lay a substantial Arverni garrison, capable of easily holding its ramparts against most assaults. Surveying the fortress, Caesar quickly realized that the majority of Gergovia's logistics were kept atop a nearby hill, rather than within the fort itself. In a daring night assault, the Romans took this hill, and secured for themselves the defender's caches of grain, munitions and water. Desperate, Vercingetorix attempted to weaken the Roman resolve through other means. He appealed to Caesar's longtime allies, the Aedui. The Aedui had increasingly become alienated from Caesar as a result of his recent conquests, and were wary of Rome's increasing curtailment of Gallic independence. Many of their nobles were easily won over to Vercingetorix' cause, persuaded as they were by his gold and promises of autonomy. The Aedui contingent broke off from Caesar's main force and attacked his supply lines, placing the Roman siege into great jeopardy. Caesar turned to contend with the Aedui army, and left behind two legions to continue to besiege Gergovia. Roman manpower thus divided, the beleaguered Arverni attacked the fortifications. The Romans struggled to repel their onslaught. At the same time, Caesar successfully surrounded and defeated the Aedui rebels before returning to Gergovia — despite large parts of the Aedui nation continuing to revolt against Rome. He needed to draw Vercingetorix from the high ground, and attempted to pull him from the fortifications through use of a decoy retreat. However, during the chaos of the fighting, a portion of Caesar's army was unaware of the general order to retreat. Motivated by what they perceived to be a weakening defense of Gergovia, these soldiers pressed onwards to the city and began sacking and plundering it. Vercingetorix and the Gauls became aware of the commotion that emanated behind them, and rushed back to the fortress. Caesar was now powerless to assist those legionaries who were now trapped behind Gergovia's walls. Of Roman losses, 46 centurions and 700 legionaries were killed, with several thousand others wounded. This was compared to the several hundred Gallic losses. Forced to withdraw from his siege, Gergovia marked a significant defeat for Caesar.

Despite his opponent's defeat at Gergovia, Vercingetorix decided not to pursue Caesar. He believed that the timing was not right for a major Gallic offensive, and refused to endanger his victory without the full support of his allies. In doing so, Vercingetorix had effectively abandoned the Aedui to Caesar's wrath. Vercingetorix instead chose to regroup at the city of Alesia: a fortress ringed by rivers and valleys, with strong battlements that proved insurmountable in a frontal assault. Sensing his opponent's hesitancy, Caesar resolved to first punish the Aedui for their betrayal. In doing so, he would also secure his rear supply lines before resuming battle with the Arverni. His punitive expedition was swift and brutal: the Aedui rebellious nobility capitulated after a token defense of their capital of Bibracte. The Aedui defeated, Caesar wasted no time bringing the fight to the Arverni. Upon his arrival at Alesia, he learned that a significant garrison of 80,000 men manned the city. To reduce the number of Roman casualties, Caesar opted for a prolonged siege of the fortress — hoping to wear the defenders out by chipping away at their supplies. Given the large size of the garrison, this would have provided a swift resolution to the rebellion. To allow for the success of his siege, Caesar constructed a ring of fortifications around the city of Alesia, circumvallating it with watchtowers, trenches and walls. The Arverni would not allow these defenses to be built uncontested: they made repeated charges at the Roman engineers in an attempt to halt their efforts, but Caesar's light skirmishers were capable of warding off such attacks with minimal delays. Caesar also ordered the construction of a second wall designed to protect the Roman rear. This was done not only to discourage the defenders inside, but also to protect his legions should a relieving army attempt to dislodge Caesar from his position. To an observer, the siege of Alesia therefore resembled a ring of fortifications, as one side sought to better ensnare the other. The beleaguered Gauls, now faced with worsening conditions with the closing of their supply lines, sought to evacuate their women and children from the fortress on Alesia. Perhaps they hoped that Caesar would feel benevolent and allow them to leave unscathed. However, Caesar would offer no such quarter, and ordered that nothing was to be done for the Gallic civilians who were trapped between the walls of Alesia and those of the Romans. This provides a striking example of the depths of Caesar's capacity for cruelty. With such a spectacle clearly visible to the Gallic defenders, their morale began to fail. Many contemplated surrender to Caesar. Vercingetorix himself contemplated offering himself in exchange for his people. At this moment of crisis, a relieving army headed by Commius, the Belgic king of the Atrebates, appeared on the horizon. This host postured against Caesar's fortifications, and began besieging the Romans from the rear. The Roman besiegers had themselves become the besieged. Vercingetorix simultaneously ordered an attack upon Caesar's front to coincide with the assault led by Commius. This failed, but the Gallic resolve had been strengthened upon witnessing the arrival of their allies. What ensued was a multitude of attacks on Caesar's fortifications, each in turn being repelled by the complexity of the Roman defenses and the siege technology they employed. Using accurate fire from scorpions and ballistae, the Romans pushed back their attackers. Yet Commius' armies pushed on, forcing Caesar to concede a portion of his fortifications. At this juncture, it was only thanks to the efforts of the Roman cavalry that saved the Roman army from defeat, and bought them the opportunity to reclaim their palisades. The Romans were victorious, but remained exhausted from the fresh onslaught.

However, during this most recent battle, the Gauls had learned of a section of Caesar's walls that was incomplete and vulnerable to attack. The very next day, Vercassivellaunus, cousin to Vercingetorix, led the relieving army's assault upon this external weakness. An Arverni onslaught from Alesia simultaneously attacked the inner fortifications. Pressed against such overwhelming numbers, the Romans could do nothing but form ranks and stand their ground. Caesar himself strode alongside the front ranks of his soldiers, yelling words of encouragement as they fought against the blitz of Gallic warriors. Labienus was tasked with holding the furthest breach in the fortifications. It was there that the heaviest of the fighting occurred, and the Roman soldiers holding these palisades were swiftly beginning to buckle under the sheer number of attackers. Desperate, Caesar formed his cavalry and pushed outside the front gates of his fortifications, whirling the 6,000 horsemen under his command around the walls so as to strike at the Gauls from their rear. Surprised at the brazenness of Caesar, Labienus' section quickly regained their spirits and redoubled their efforts against the Gauls. Pressed against the legionaries' swords from within the fortifications, and the spears of the Roman cavalry behind — the Gallic relieving army lost all hope and broke. The fear created by the routing warriors spread swiftly through the Gauls' ranks, seizing each man until a general rout formed. The chaotic disarray that resulted allowed for the Romans to swiftly and easily cut the Gauls down as they ran. The slaughter was terrible: Caesar's soldiers cut through them without mercy, hacking at any Gaul that fell within arm's reach. Caesar famously remarked that it was only the exhaustion of his legions that prevented the utter annihilation of the Gauls at Alesia. Having witnessed the great suffering and slaughter of his people, Vercingetorix promptly surrendered to Caesar — famously stripping himself of his arms and armor until he kneeled, chest bare, before the conqueror. Upon the fields of Alesia in 52 BC, the Celtic supremacy of Gaul had been brought to an end. Caesar stood triumphant over his defeated foe, and cast an eye south towards Rome, where his enemies conspired his ruin.

Chapter 5: Pompey in Rome

Julius Caesar's conquest of Gaul was the defining event of the First Triumvirate. Through his efforts, the Roman dominion not only greatly expanded its holdings in the North, but also filled its coffers with plunder and the proceeds from sales of Gallic slaves. What was necessary to drive such military success was that the Senate be incapable of removing Caesar from power. Caesar's fantastic conquests drew considerable attention to his persona, and many of his opponents sought to have him removed from command and brought to trial for his previous illegal activities. His debts and instances of corruption were raised by the *optimates*. Central in driving away such indictments were the efforts of Gnaeus Pompey Magnus, the Triumvir charged with overseeing the affairs of the alliance in Rome.

Pompey Magnus profited tremendously from his alliance with both Caesar and Crassus. Due to Caesar's appointment to the consulship, Pompey had successfully managed to find land for his veterans. Moreover, he diligently performed his duties as overseer of the Roman grain supply — refusing the governorship of Hispania Ulterior to remain within the city. His acumen as leader secured, Pompey could then resign himself to enjoying his phenomenal success alongside his new wife, Julia. As a pillar of the Triumvirate, Pompey was untouchable in the eyes of the Senate. Together, the alliance had succeeded in winning over the city of Rome to their interests. They had sufficiently demonstrated that any opposition on behalf of the *optimates* would undoubtedly result in exile, due to their possession of Clodius as Tribune of the Plebs. It was through Clodius that the alliance was capable of instigating its sweeping reforms. It was through Clodius that they intimidated their many enemies. Clodius formed an underpinning to their alliance that proved useful beyond their wildest dreams. His armed gangs roamed the streets of Rome, swiftly executing any of their opponents in a clandestine, but chillingly visible manner. His men would shout down notable politicians, and shower them with stones and projectiles. They even threatened arson against their property. Pompey was wary of the consequences of partaking in such tactics, but was encouraged by its success in both cowing and winning over volatile senators to their faction.

Clodius, however, was gradually becoming dissatisfied with his station of servitude to the Triumvirate. The success of his attacks against Cicero had fueled his ambition. Wielding Tribunician powers, Clodius believed himself to be beyond reproach, and saw himself as capable of negotiating with the strongest men of Rome on equal terms. This drew the ire of Pompey Magnus, who, in 58 BC, began criticizing Clodius' increasingly unabashed attempts at conferring political power. While Caesar pursued his military campaigns in Gaul, Pompey began to suggest the possibility of recalling Cicero from exile, a suggestion that greatly infuriated Clodius. The latter responded by harassing Pompey: a gesture that was supported in secret by Marcus Licinius Crassus. Despite their alliance, Crassus and Pompey continued to hold animosity towards one another. This resentment risked untangling their Triumvirate now that Caesar was preoccupied elsewhere in the world. Motivated by Crassus, Clodius finally unleashed his thugs against Pompey when he moved to recall Cicero. The assassination attempt against Pompey failed, but succeeded in throwing Rome into a period of violent flux. Clodius' attacks became so frequent that they succeeded in confining Pompey to his home until the end of the year. Pompey thus removed, Clodius turned against Caesar himself, decreeing that his consular appointment in 59 BC was illegal, and that all legislation instigated during that time was to be repealed. Caesar ignored this, dismissing Clodius as a nuisance. However, this blunt disregard succeeding only in upsetting Clodius more. As the other tribunes voted for the recall of Cicero, Clodius attempted to block the legislation through use of the Tribunician's veto power. He succeeded. Nonetheless, Caesar gave his tacit approval for the reintroduction of Cicero's recall following the conclusion of Clodius' term as Tribune at the end of 58 BC. The subsequent attempts to pass such a bill were blocked by violence, as Clodius' gangs renewed attacks in January of 57 BC upon senatorial property. They engaged in acts of brutality to demonstrate their possession of the Roman streets. To combat the rogue Tribune, Pompey gave Clodius' rivals, Titus Annius Milo and Publius Sestius, the approval to raise armed gangs of their own. These gangs were often stocked with former slaves and other poor men, who each fought for their patron's interests with the hopes of securing future advancement. Some of these gangs were even comprised of gladiators, lending the thugs a certain professionalism that made them valuable enforcers. As a result of Pompey's appointments, open gang warfare consumed the streets of Rome for much of 57 BC as Milo and Sestius sought to weaken Clodius' hold. They were successful, and Cicero's recall was passed in the Senate in the latter half of the year.

Infuriated at his loss in influence, Clodius began to personally attack the benefactors that sought to bring back Cicero to power. He attacked the workmen who were rebuilding the destroyed home of the former exile, and even tried killing Cicero on the streets of Rome. Caesar's lieutenant, Quintus Tullius Cicero, was not spared the vengeance so desired upon his brother, and Clodius burned down his home. It is readily apparent that Roman politics had developed a clandestine element that verged on open warfare. Through using these gangs, both Clodius and the Triumvirate were guilty of seeking to remove the other from power. However, due to the fact that power dictated the law, neither individual was capable of being charged with having committed a heinous offence, despite Cicero repeatedly trying to use the Roman judicial system to bring them to justice. It became evident that during the period of vicious street brawls, the Roman judicial system had degenerated into a travesty.

While the streets of Rome were embroiled in incessant violence between supporters of Clodius and those of Milo, the mutual understanding that held together the Triumvirate began to fray. Increasingly, Pompey's friends tried to convince him that Crassus sought his assassination. Both men were envious of Caesar's recent successes in Gaul, and despised that they were not the ones to benefit from such a military campaign. Distrust fomented to such an extent that it threatened the very foundation of the alliance. Concerned, Caesar called together a meeting of the three in the northern Italian town of Luca in 56 BC. There, they discussed the future of the alliance. The machinations of Clodius had done much to weaken the bonds of mutual respect that the members of the Triumvirate had previously held for one another. It was necessary that the three meet and discuss in person — away from the chaos that was then consuming Rome. Plutarch describes how each brought their associated clients, so that the city of Luca became filled with some one hundred and twenty lictors and two hundred senators. It was a monumental meeting: the strongest men in Rome were dictating the future of the city. They agreed that the consulship of 55 BC was to be held by Caesar and Pompey. Moreover, they agreed that Caesar's command in Gaul would be extended by another five years, so as to provide him with additional protection against those who sought judicial action. Pompey would continue to govern over Spain as his jurisdiction, whereupon he could continue the work he had begun decades before of creating a stable Roman presence within the province. Upon the conclusion of their joint consulship, Crassus was to be given the praetorship of Syria — a lucrative and highly desired position. There, Crassus would be capable of best monitoring his clients in the East. Moreover, he would be capable of launching his own campaign against the Parthian Empire — a campaign he so ardently desired. Some opponents attempted to criticize the decrees created by the Luca conference, but were rapidly dismissed by widespread disapproval on the part of the senators, who each sought to gain the approval of the Triumvirate. The meeting concluded, Caesar returned to Gaul, and Pompey and Crassus departed for Rome.

The return of Pompey and Crassus created a commotion within the city. Its very atmosphere was rife with suspicion as the *optimates* sought to understand what conclusions had been reached at the meeting in Luca. Of these, Pompey and Crassus conceded nothing. For instance, when asked if Pompey would run for the consulship, he replied that he might, or he might not. Crassus replied to the same question in a similar way. Such was their replies that the leaders of the opposing factions became emboldened at the prospect of themselves becoming consul. Such secrecy is understandable. With enemies as brutal as Clodius, secrecy was a necessity for the success of the Triumvirate's plan. However, when it became time for Pompey and Crassus to announce their candidature, their opponents took flight. Only one *optimate* attempted to compete with the Triumvirs, a friend of Cato's by the name of Domitius. Domitius was encouraged by the widespread support he received among many of the Triumvirate's enemies. Disturbed by the success of his candidature, Pompey and Crassus had their supporters harass and attack those of Domitius', so much so that members of the candidate's entourage were murdered in the streets. Moreover, to further tip the scales in their favor and bring the decisions made at the Luca conference into reality, both Caesar and Pompey had Rome flooded with their supporters. Soldiers who had been fighting for Caesar in Gaul were sent to Rome to cast their vote in support of the Triumvirate, and Pompey's veterans were roused from their farm work. The result was that the consular election of 55 BC was a resounding success for the faction, with each member being assigned exactly what he wanted. Pompey had control of both Hispania Ulterior and Citerior; Crassus was given the praetorship in Syria, and Caesar continued to earn his string of victories while campaigning in Gaul.

Some contemporary historians have posited that there might have been an ulterior motive behind the Luca conference. Plutarch documents that Caesar had himself become increasingly suspicious of his allies within the Triumvirate. His reasons for holding the conference were less to do with strengthening the Triumvirate, and were more concerned with ascertaining the strengths of both Pompey and Crassus. It is possible that Caesar was determining where he himself might stand should the alliance fall apart. It is true that Plutarch had the gift of hindsight, however we should note that there are considerable truths to many of his claims. Caesar was in fact using his conquest of Gaul as a means of both advancing his personal interests, but also to create ties of loyalty between himself and his soldiers. These soldiers were becoming highly skilled and experienced. Moreover, he was continuously sending vast amounts of plunder back to Rome. These treasures were then used to buy himself allies and friends both among the Senate and the greater Roman populace. Plutarch documents that it had been Caesar — not so much Pompey or Crassus — who had drawn such vast crowds to Luca. The Roman elite was curious of his successes beyond the Alps, and was eager to lay eyes upon the man who had won so much for Rome in so short a period of time. At Luca, Caesar gave gifts and grants to each man who swore support to his cause. Gifts such as these were vital in creating friends and allies in Rome. Such a course of action can only be interpreted as prudent. It is evident that Caesar was not seeking the demise of his allies, but rather looking for reassurances of support among the Roman elite that would have provided the protection necessary to ensure his survival in the ensuing struggle for power should the Triumvirate fall.

It is evident that the successes of the Luca conference and the offices it secured on behalf of the Triumvirate were necessary to maintaining the alliance. It consolidated the trust each man had for the other, and thus bought the alliance more time during a period of tremendous political volatility. 55 BC saw the continuation of the violent trend that had begun under Clodius. Now, however, there were new players. Rome had become a physical battlefield, as rival gangs vied with one another to either curb or protect the political capabilities of the Triumvirs. Following Caesar and Pompey's terms of office as consul in 55 BC, Crassus and Pompey were in turn to share another joint consulship. The shared rule of the Triumvirate monopolized the most important curial office within the Roman state, and the alliance between Crassus, Pompey and Caesar seemed completely invulnerable.

Chapter 6: Crassus in Syria

Marcus Licinius Crassus was overjoyed when he first learned of the Triumvirate's success in securing the provincial appointments. His previously modest and mild temperament changed when he acquired Syria as his consular province. Following his appointment, Crassus became a braggart who assumed an air of superiority over his contemporaries. He told everyone, regardless of station, that he would lead the most successful command Rome had ever seen in the East. His claims were not without merit: Syria was among the wealthiest province in the Roman Empire. Situated on the Mediterranean coast near the Levant, Syria had been traditionally under the sway of the ancient Persian Empire. Its conquest by Macedonia had allowed for its consolidation under Alexander the Great's successor, Seleucus I, during the period of incessant civil wars that followed Alexander's death. The Seleucid Kingdom had reigned over an exceedingly rich territory. Syria was a lush, densely urbanized region, which made the collection of taxation an easy practice. With its conquest by Pompey Magnus in the late Republic, Rome brought its system of taxation and collection into Syria. It was the same system that had previously been applied to Asia Minor. These tax collectors were extremely corrupt. They bribed Roman officials by the thousands to secure the most lucrative placements throughout the East. Since Pompey's conquest, successive governors of Syria had become phenomenally rich as a result of their tenure in office. However, the promise of wealth presented but one facet as to why Crassus was so excited for his command in Syria. Wealth could not have been his only motivation, given Crassus' already substantial fortune. He was, after all, the wealthiest man in Rome.

It is evident that what Crassus desired most in Syria was the prospect of leading a vast military campaign. While in Rome, he boasted loudly of his plans for such an impending conquest. Crassus had set his eyes on a campaign that would rival that led by Alexander centuries earlier. He wanted to conquer the Levant, to bring Bactria and the Indus Valley into the Roman fold. He dreamed of a Roman dominion that stretched from the coasts of Spain to the banks of the Indian Ocean. His conquest was to be grand, with tremendous potential for wealth and plunder. He wanted to subjugate kings and bring down empires. That such potential exist was imperative. The Gauls were all but subjugated, leaving the targets of future Roman conquest to be found only in the East. Crassus had belittled the campaigns of his rivals, Pompey and Caesar, declaring that they would pale in comparison to the future successes he would achieve while East. He had been envious of Caesar's mounting popularity in the wake of his Gallic successes. When compared to the other members of the Triumvirate, Crassus had the least military accolades to his name. He was perpetually aware of this fact. He was therefore hungry to gain some degree of martial glory so that he might compete with his colleagues. To reinforce his status as foremost citizen of Rome, Crassus set his sights on the vast Parthian Empire: the descendents of Achaemenid Persia.

Many Romans were concerned at the idea of a Roman war with Parthia. To the public, Parthia was a Roman ally in the East, a mysterious nation that had committed no hostility against the Roman people or its friends. Stable diplomatic relations with Parthia were necessary for Rome to continue pursuing its commercial enterprises with the kingdoms of the Indus Valley and the Chinese Empire that lay beyond. They stood opposed to any conflict with the Parthian Empire. In contrast to this popular opposition to Crassus' bellicosity, both Triumvirs greatly encouraged their partner. Caesar, in particular, was most supportive of Crassus' plan, writing him frequently with words of encouragement from Gaul. He commended Crassus' resolution, and further incited him to war. It is evident that Caesar was concerned with the possibility of a strained Triumvirate. Caesar was aware that he stood alone in Gaul, while both Crassus and Pompey remained in Rome. Should a break have occurred between the three, it was possible that both Crassus and Pompey could have temporarily reconciled their differences and formed an allied opposition against Caesar. What was necessary was the gift of a command to each Triumvir — a distraction to occupy their time. Pompey had his wife, Julia; Crassus had his provincial command in Syria.

Buoyed by both Caesar and Pompey, Crassus set his departure for Syria in the latter half of 55 BC. However, upon attempting to leave the city, he discovered Ateius, a Tribune of the Plebs, barring his way. Ateius was staunchly opposed to Crassus' expedition in Syria. He feared the divine repercussions of a Roman campaign in Asia, and gathered many supporters to assist him in preventing Crassus from leaving Rome. Ateius firmly was convinced of the necessity of *jus bellum*, believing that Rome could only be victorious if it fought a morally justified conflict. To Ateius, a war with Parthia concerned itself not with justice, but avarice and greed. Fearing the growing mob, Crassus appealed to Pompey to join him as he departed from the city. He sought the safety that Pompey provided. Crassus knew that Pompey was widely beloved by the common folk because he had won them so many victories. He also knew that the people would not attempt to physically halt Crassus lest they desired to move Pompey to anger. With his colleague at his side, Crassus succeeded in leaving the city of Rome — being harangued only once at the city's gates. There stood Ateius, who stoked a sacred fire and uttered an ancient and dark curse on Crassus' name. The consequences of this act were felt by all, with the public believing that the curse fell not only upon Crassus, but also on the entirety of Rome. Crassus departed from the port of Brundisium with due haste, risking the dangerous waters of the Mediterranean Sea late in the year. His desire for expediency resulted in the loss of many vessels on his journey. This was a frequent occurrence. Shipwrecks in Republican times were so commonplace that there existed insurance companies tasked with protecting businessmen and traders from loss, should there occur a wreck. Arriving in Asia Minor, Crassus marched through the Kingdom of Galatia to meet with its monarch, King Deiotarus, who was engaged in the construction of a new city. The Roman biographer, Plutarch, documents how Crassus remarked that he found it strange that the king had undertaken new constructions at such an advanced age. Deiotarus famously replied that neither did Crassus undertake his Parthian expedition very early —referring to Crassus' own sixty years. Crassus dismissed this rebuke, stating that he could still wield a sword well enough. He marched peacefully through Galatia and immediately began his campaign by crossing over the Euphrates. The Roman invasion had taken the Parthian Empire entirely by surprise: his forces quickly overwhelmed the cities of Mesopotamia, many of them surrendering to Crassus' voluntarily. The city of Zenodotia proved more challenging. There, the Romans suffered a slight setback that resulted in the deaths of over a hundred men. Upset at this minor loss, Crassus resolved for a violent offensive, in which he successfully took the city by storm, setting the heads of its defenders atop the city's parapets. Crassus celebrated his victory over the Zenodotians by having his troops hail him as an *imperator*. Reveling in his latest success, Crassus returned to Syria for the winter, and left behind a small garrison in Mesopotamia to guard his newest conquests. His son, Publius Licinius Crassus — a decorated veteran who had served alongside Caesar — rejoined him in Asia Minor, bringing with him one thousand elite horsemen.

In choosing to return to winter quarters, Crassus had committed the first major blunder of his campaign. His retirement for the season allowed the gargantuan Parthian Empire to mobilize its armies and consolidate its holdings in the Levant. This would prevent further betrayals from taking place in the disillusioned cities of Babylon and Selucia, who still held pro-Roman sentiments. Such cities were vital for supply and logistics purposes, as they were oasis amidst the surrounding desert. Moreover, had he approached, these cities would have easily supported Crassus and expelled their Parthian garrisons. However, it is noted that instead of conquest, Crassus spent his winter more like a usurer than a general. He counted the vast treasures of Syria, and levied taxation upon the subjugated cities. This earned him the spite of many of his soldiers, who probably came to expect conquests akin to those enjoyed by Caesar. Crassus' behavior should come as no surprise. Although he came to Syria with the intention of embarking upon a military conquest, Crassus' also had his official obligation to govern the province. His extensive experience made him competent in financial affairs, and provided him with an opportunity to serve his burgeoning clientele of tax collectors in the East. One could speculate that the frustration felt by his legions was likely due to the popular belief that he had retired from the season's fighting too early.

When he withdrew his army from winter quarters in 53 BC, a Parthian ambassador met Crassus and asked what Rome's intent was in conducting an invasion of their lands. The ambassador wished to know whether it was the popular decision of the Roman people, or a mere military exercise undertaken for Crassus' gain. Crassus stated that the ambassador would have his response when his legions marched on Selucia. The ambassador quickly ascertained Crassus' true purpose: avarice, or the pursuit of riches. Crassus sought to enrich the Roman state at the expense of the Parthian Empire, thereby winning him the same love of the people enjoyed by Caesar and Pompey. He wanted equity in the adulation from his city. Nevertheless, the ambassador's words bolstered the swelling fear amongst the Roman ranks. Soldiers who had escaped earlier from the garrisons fighting in Mesopotamia had previously sewed this sentiment. They spoke of the sheer vastness of the Parthian host, and of the terrifying way in which it conducted warfare. These men described the Parthian soldiers and how they fought with a terrible speed, mounted as they were on horseback. They shot projectiles that could pierce any armor, and wielded maces and axes that easily clove Roman shields. Their armor was unlike any before seen by Roman eyes.

The Roman garrison's surprise was due to them having mistakenly assumed that the Parthians would be similar to the Armenians or the Cappadocians. These peoples had been conquered earlier, and had fled in droves before the onslaught of the Roman legions. The soldiers had followed Crassus under the pretense that the most challenging aspect of the campaign would be the march. Now, having witnessed this new foe, they had doubts as to the success of their efforts.

The Parthian state was a product of its environment. Its ruling dynasty was the Arsacid family, who reigned over the expanse of its dominions from their seat in Ctesiphon. The Empire was phenomenally wealthy, however, the first century BC was a time of particular domestic instability for the Arsacids as Parthian nobles vied with their monarch for power. Situated in the heart of the Iranian plateau, the Parthians possessed a long tradition of horse mastery that they used to assert dominance over their neighbors. Their armies were oriented so as to best contend with their fiercest rivals: the Scythians. Being a tribal confederacy of nomads from the Asiatic Steppes, the Scythians preferred archery from atop horses. To protect themselves from Scythian incursions, it became necessary for the Parthians to adopt a similar technique of warfare. Therefore, Parthian armies by the first century BC were largely composed of horse archers, who were lightly armored and wielded composite bows. These bows had tremendous striking power and could pierce most contemporary armor and shields with great ease. The horse archers gave Parthian forces great flexibility and mobility during battle. Parthian infantry typically favored light armaments, as well. Adorned in cloth and leather, Parthian infantry predominately wielded spears and bows and fought in looser formations than their Roman counterparts. The central element in such a troop composition was speed, allowing the Parthian host to weave in and out of battle and exploit the advantages its ranged elements provided. Perhaps the most formidable component of the Parthian army was its cataphracts. These formidable horsemen were very well the shock cavalry of the ancient world. Armored entirely in sheet mail, the Parthian cataphract rode a war steed that was itself covered in metal plating. Due to the weight of this protection, the Parthian horses were much larger and stockier than those of Italian or Greek breeds. Cataphracts wielded lances upon the charge, with which they used to break into densely compacted enemy infantry formations. Once engaged in battle, the cataphract typically favored the armor penetrating capabilities provided by blunt weapons such as maces and war axes. The sheer cost of the horses, armor and weapons worn by a cataphract meant that they belonged to the upper echelon of Parthian society. It is apparent that the devastating charges of the cataphract, combined with the versatility of the horse archer, made the Parthian army a force to truly be reckoned with.

Despite this new information, Crassus remained resolute in his plans of conquering the Parthian Empire. He approached the Armenian king, Artabazes, with his designs, and was given support in the form of a contingent of six thousand horsemen — a little more than a petty kings-guard. Artabazes had earlier promised to Crassus an army of ten thousand Armenian knights, in addition to thirty thousand footmen.

Thus, his grant of support came as a disappointment to Crassus, who had expected more soldiers. Not wanting to disappoint his Roman guest, Artabazes offered Crassus' strategic advice, suggesting that he attack Parthia from his kingdom. He would allow the Romans free passage through his lands, as well as grants of provisions and supply wherever they were in the kingdom. His suggestion was sound. By remaining in Armenia, Crassus' legions would be protected from incursion by Parthian cavalry by the topography. Armenia had vast mountains and high valley passes, which served as an impediment to horsemen. Crassus received this knowledge with a cold thanks, but stubbornly adhered to his original plan of marching over the flatlands of Mesopotamia to retrieve his units stationed in garrisons throughout the region. He would then undertake his invasion of Parthia by way of the Iranian plateau. Disappointed at his counterpart's obstinate response, Artabazes wished him the utmost success in his enterprise, and the two parted ways. Crassus' army crossed the river at Zeugma and set about constructing a camp. The Roman army was in poor spirits; each of their portents had proved unfavorable to the expedition. Moreover, the constitution of the Roman army was severely lacking and a poor match for the terrain they marched through. He had under his command seven legions of heavy infantry, three thousand skirmishers, and a little less than four thousand horsemen.

As they marched, the Roman scouts closely monitored the terrain ahead of the army, always searching for the enemy. They discovered evidence of the Parthians everywhere: coming across the hoof prints of innumerable horses that seemed to be fleeing before the advance of the Roman army. Hearing this, Crassus became greatly emboldened and began to despise his Parthian enemies. He claimed that they were incapable of meeting a Roman host in combat. He wanted to decisively defeat the Parthian war effort, and so hoped to soon meet their army in battle to demonstrate his prowess as general.

However, the Parthians continued to elude him. Whereas Crassus' strategy was to overwhelm the western cities of the Empire and win them over as Roman client states, the Parthians sought to cut Crassus off from his supplies. They would engage the Romans in battle only when the situation required it.

The catalyst for the inevitable first confrontation between the Romans and the Parthians was an Osreone chief by the name of Ariamnes. Ariamnes was known to Rome, as he had been a friend of Pompey when the latter was conquering the Seleucid kingdom. Therefore, Ariamnes held the title of friend to the Romans, and was wholeheartedly trusted by Crassus. Ariamnes approached the Roman general, praising him for the size and effectiveness of his legions. He declared himself an ally of Pompey's, and asked why Crassus was delaying to press on against the Parthians. When Crassus did not reply, Ariamnes declared that it was obvious that the Parthians would never meet the Romans in battle, and that the Romans could easily take the Parthian fortresses from their cowardly foes. Ariamnes had a persuasive tongue, and he found a willing listener in Crassus. He spoke of the paltry defense set up by the Parthian generals, Surena and Silaces, and of the weakness of their armies. These were all lies, however. Ariamnes had long been in the service of Parthia, and was then serving Surena, who hoped to alienate the Romans from their allies, and slowly wear them down in the desert. While this was happening, Silaces would punish King Artabazes of Armenia for his transgressions. The Parthian strategy was therefore a delaying tactic. Surena was given a small force with which he was to draw the Romans further and further into the Mesopotamian desert, while Silaces was charged with defeating the Armenians. Silaces would then regroup with Surena, and receive reinforcements from the larger Parthian host, which would then crush Crassus' army. Ariamnes role was to instigate this first battle, so that Crassus could become emboldened by his supposed victory and lose sight of the greater events taking place around him.

The Parthian general Surena was no ordinary man. He came from a family of great renown in the empire, and was deemed the bravest man in all of Persia by Roman historians. His retinue matched his status, and everywhere he went a baggage troop of one thousand camels, two hundred concubines, a bodyguard of one thousand soldiers, and ten thousand horsemen followed him. Some rightly posit that Surena was a rival of the Parthian king, Hyrodes, in terms of splendor and magnificence. Such an explanation is sensible given the context of the Arsacid decline in the first century BC. The nobility had been undermining the power of the Arsacid monarchy, creating fear of revolution among the ruling family. With this knowledge in mind, the appointment of Surena as head of a paltry force was therefore the result of such power politics. Hyrodes wanted to rid himself of Surena by placing him at the head of a small army charged with acting as bait for the Romans. Such an appointment would likely result in a zero-win situation, where Surena would be either killed or dishonored by defeat. Surena would be significantly reduced in status or removed from power altogether. The Parthian general was undoubtedly aware of such maneuverings, and likely sought to orient his forces in such a way as to ensure victory. Hence, his use of Ariamnes as an agent.

It was Ariamnes who succeeded in convincing Crassus to follow him, and he led the Roman army from the safety of the Euphrates River into the vast plains of the Mesopotamian desert. There, the Romans found themselves on an even terrain that was best suited for the horsemen that fought in the Parthian style. Their army was led ever further into the heart of the desert and away from their supply line, moving until there was nothing on the horizon but sand. Whispers of treachery spanned the army, and the legions began to suspect Ariamnes. Many believed that he had been secretly working for the Parthians, and that his purpose was to intentionally mislead them. A messenger from Artabazes reached Crassus, and warned them of an attack that had taken place on Armenia. He beseeched that they turn back and join the defense of the kingdom against the Parthians. Ariamnes dismissed this possibility, stating that the Armenians were a self-serving people who sought to exploit Roman dominance in the region at Crassus' expense. He exhorted the Romans with claims that they had nearly passed the desert and reached the heartlands of Assyria — the soft underbelly of Parthia. Hearing this, Crassus dismissed the messenger.

The legions marched on, increasingly bitter at the ever-worsening conditions as they finally arrived at a point in the desert where there was no water or shade. Ariamnes, his deception successful, disappeared in the night — leaving the Roman host stranded amidst the sands.

Disturbed by the disappearance of his friend, Crassus sent out a group of scouts to ascertain as to the direction of his travel. From the group, only a few of the scouts returned. They were grievously wounded and bore news of a Parthian army that loomed nearby outside of the town of Carrhae. This discovery sent Crassus into a state of panic. Ariamnes had betrayed him. His soldiers had been right. He hastened to form his army into a proper formation. Having obtained some semblance of marching order, Crassus drew his courage and marched towards Carrhae. Learning that the Parthian forces there were a paltry few thousand in number, he determined that his first victory against the Parthian army was to occur here. Crassus' legate, Cassius, suggested that he form his army into a *triplex acies* so as to bolster their ranks and improve their mobility. Such a formation would also discourage charges by the Parthian horsemen. Crassus was instead wary of the Parthian horse archers, and changed his formation into a hollow square. This formation would allow the Romans to repel attacks launched from any side, at expense to the army's mobility. The Parthians continued their gradual retreat away from the Romans, and skirted the conflict by remaining just outside of the reach of their projectiles.

Thus, the day was spent in slow pursuit, with the Romans struggling through the heat and the sands to meet their Parthian enemies. They marched forward under a persistent barrage of fire, and the arrows and spears of the Parthians often piercing shields, and, sometimes, a man. As the day drew to its end, the Romans arrived at a stream where Cassius advised Crassus to build his camp beside to allow his men to rest. Recharged from a night's sleep, his army would have been better capable of fighting its highly maneuverable enemies. Crassus contemplated this for a time, aware that their current position was too exposed and ideal for Parthian missile fire. It was his son, Publius, who had the final say on Crassus' decision. Publius, at the head of his division of Gallic cavalry, was insatiable in his desire for conquest. Publius had earlier distinguished himself in Gaul serving under Caesar, and had long become accustomed to the tremendous victories that had been gained there. Publius believed that the Parthians were in a state of extreme weakness, and that a push on the part of the Romans would be all that was necessary to send their Empire into capitulation. With such words he urged his father, and told him that an assault was necessary. Accepting his son's advice, Crassus reformed his army into a hollow square and continued towards Surena. Aware that he was rapidly running out of land, the Parthian *spahbod* prepared to meet the Romans in conflict. He orchestrated a number of acts that were designed to intimidate and further demoralized his enemies. The Parthians beat a number of drums, and the Parthians cataphracts — carrying light garments — conducted a false charge on the Roman lines, only to break off at the last minute and shed their clothes to reveal the extent of their armor in front of their enemies. The Romans, firmly disciplined, were not remotely phased by such gestures. They merely stood in formation and awaited the inevitable charge of the Parthian horsemen. Dismayed, Surena changed his tactics. Instead of leading with a cavalry charge, Surena decided to use his horse archers to continue wearing away at the Roman lines. Surrounding the Roman body, the Parthian horse archers fired at Crassus' soldiers with impunity. Seeking to halt the near-incessant stream of arrows, Crassus ordered his skirmishers to march out beyond the lines to return fire. The skirmishers attempted to accomplish this, but their arrows fell short of striking the horsemen. They chased after the Parthians for a time, but the horse archers would wheel about, and firing from a safe distance.

Standing before the ranks of the Roman heavy infantry, Crassus' skirmishers were shot to pieces, their light armaments provided no defense against the heavy shot. They were all but annihilated when a surprise charge by Surena's cataphracts smote them down where they stood. Despairing the loss of a portion of his army and sensing the futility of their endeavor, Crassus ordered his legionnaires forward. Surena's horse archers turned to strike them, instead. Although deadly to light infantry, the horse archers proved less effective against the rows of heavily shielded and armored legionaries. Contemporary accounts are conflicted on the effectiveness of the Parthian arrows: some posit that the Roman's armor provided complete coverage, while others argued that missiles pierced through the shields to embed themselves in the limbs and other extremities. Under this deadly hail of arrows, the Romans pursued their quarry, proving incapable of reaching them. Exasperated with the never-ending rain of missiles, Crassus ordered his men to form into *testudo* formation: a formation created by the rigid compacting of soldiers into a box formation with their shields facing in each direction. The Roman *testudo* was excellent in sieges and during the early skirmishing phase of a pitched battle, as the interlocked shields boosted defensive capabilities and mitigated casualties from arrow fire. However, upon the sands of Carrhae, the *testudo* proved to be a tremendous hindrance to the Romans. The *testudo* was first and foremost a defensive formation. By compacting legionaries together, the *testudo* protected them from arrows and javelins at the expensive of their ability in melee combat. Moreover, by condensing so many men together in one small area, the legionaries were rendered extremely vulnerable to the thunderous charge of the Parthian cataphracts. Crassus, in giving the order for *testudo* formations, endangered thousands of his men. Surena spied this weakness and capitalized on it. Having whittled down the already beleaguered Romans with arrow fire, he ordered that the cataphracts were now to charge in and scatter those who survived. This they did, and their deadly charge sent Romans careening to and fro. The effectiveness of the cataphracts' axes was further amplified by the *testudo*. With so many men tightly packed together, it was impossible to miss bludgeoning a disoriented Roman's skull. As the survivors of each charge scrambled to spread out to fight back against the cataphracts, the latter would retreat from the engagement — their retirement being following by a renewed volley of arrows, which would again force the Romans to return to *testudo*. This would, in turn, be followed by yet another charge by the cataphracts; fighting the form of engagement that they were best suited for.

Surrounded by the bodies of dead and dying Romans, Crassus single hope lay in the possibility that the Parthians might run out of missiles to launch at the trapped Romans. However, Surena had planned for such an eventuality, and had commissioned reinforcement by camel train. It was thousands of camels long, and resupplied the Parthian army with no difficulty. His horse archers could fire with impunity, striking any man who stumbled or staggered outside of formation. Increasingly desperate, Crassus ordered a charge of the Roman horse, led by his son Publius. Publius was tasked with driving off the horse archers, so that the Roman infantry might be relieved from the missiles. Publius took this with great seriousness, and enveloped himself with his 1,300 strong Gallic bodyguard. The Roman horse charged out from within the hollow square, and set themselves upon the Parthian horse archers. The archers, being a lighter cavalry unit, easily outpaced the smaller, heavier Roman cavalry. Harassing them with arrows fired in Parthian shot, the horse archers successfully led Publius far enough astray that he became isolated from the Roman lines. There, the horse archers enveloped the Roman cavalry, shooting them to pieces while they circled around, their movements concealing the slow, measured advance of the Parthian cataphracts from the main battle line. When they manifested through the spiraling dust kicked up by the horses' hooves, it was too late for the already struggling Roman cavalry. The armored cataphracts charged into Publius' unit in wedge formation, and used their sheer mass to tear into the enemy ranks and crush the lighter Roman cavalry underfoot. The Romans proved incapable of fighting back, their lances shattering upon contact with the heavy mail of the Parthians. Many were slaughtered on first contact. The rest had their horses hacked out from under them by the brutal axes of the cataphracts. Terrified, Publius and the surviving Gauls fled to the shelter of a small hilltop, but were pursued by the horse archers. There, they valiantly fought to their last breath. Yet the ferocious warriors of the West could not match the stalwart armor of the East. Although the Gauls fought gallantly, the superiority of the Parthian cavalry outmatched them. Crassus could only watch helplessly as his son's unit was cut down atop that hill. Fearing capture, Publius committed suicide rather than face the shame and dishonor of being a Parthian hostage.

Those cavalrymen who survived Surena's onslaught trickled back to the Roman lines, delivering news of the fresh defeat suffered by Publius. Fearing for his son's life, he ordered a general advance of the Roman soldiers towards the hilltop. The renewed march of the Roman line took the Parthians by surprise, and they fled from the hilltop into the plains beyond. Arriving at the scene of the slaughter, Crassus' looked desperately for signs of his son amidst the strewn bodies of Romans and Gauls. He found his head, mounted atop a spear, at the crest of the hilltop. Wracked by grief, Crassus ordered a general retreat towards the now defenseless town of Carrhae. The fleeing Roman forces hurried towards the city in a disorderly scramble, and trampled wounded legionaries underfoot as they ran. Those who fell were left behind. In all, some several thousand were left for the Parthians. Of those captured, there included several Legionary Eagles — the standards and symbols of honor borne into battle by a Roman legion. To lose one standard was considered a grievous affront within the Roman military. Losing seven was indicative of the scale of Crassus' crushing defeat. The next morning, Surena sent an embassy to Crassus to offer him a chance of surrender. In exchange for the surrender of Rome's holdings east of the Euphrates, Crassus and the Romans would be allowed to depart Parthian lands alive. Crassus was torn on his decision. His very honor was tarnished now, and there seemed to be no way to salvage his reputation from this terrible defeat. Moreover, he mourned for his dead son. His soldiers, however, had little patience for their general. They threatened mutiny should he not agree to the Parthian terms. Crassus agreed to the meeting between himself and Surena, yet during the meeting's procession, an irate Parthian soldier pulled at the reins of Crassus' horse, which provoked violence between both negotiating parties. During the conflict that ensued, Crassus and all of his generals were cut down. Upon hearing of the commotion, the remaining Roman soldiers attempted to flee

Carrhae, but most were cut down or captured as they ran. In total, some twenty thousand Romans were killed, and a further twenty thousand captured or enslaved. As punishment, Surena ordered that molten gold be poured down Crassus' throat — a fitting death for one who sought to secure the vast riches of the East for himself. Crassus' quaestor, Gaius Cassius Longinus, successfully led ten thousand survivors to the province of Syria, where they held off a vicious Parthian counterattack led by King Hyrodes.

The spectacular victory of Surena over Crassus further enhanced the Parthian general's famous reputation and appeal in Ctesiphon. In leading his paltry force of ten thousand, Surena had accomplished the impossible. He had not only halted the Roman advance, but also defeated it altogether. This greatly frustrated King Hyrodes, who had hoped to rid himself of a political rival by giving him this command. He had hoped that Crassus would kill Surena. Aware of the dangerous influence that Surena was earning within the Parthian court, Hyrodes ordered that he be executed following his victory at Carrhae.

For both empires, the Roman defeat at Carrhae in 53 BC represented a watershed. The Parthian Empire would be thrust into a vicious struggle for power between the ruling Arsacid dynasty and its rival factions. The Roman Empire, too, would feature a comparable conflict. With Crassus dead, there remained only Pompey and Caesar to act as the Triumvirate. Although long friends, the removal of Crassus would have inevitable consequences for the nature of their alliance. For a time, however, Caesar reigned peacefully in Gaul, and Pompey in Rome. Trouble brewed, but only on the distant horizon.

Chapter 7: 'Alea Jacta Est'

The death of Crassus hastened the complications that would have eventually arisen within the Triumvirate. The alliance had been designed chiefly as a means to remedy the difficulties between Pompey and Crassus. They had been the vital constituents that solidified the Triumvirate when it was first formed in 59 BC. As we have seen, Caesar was the agent who bridged their previous divisions and created the ties that now joined both men. He successfully accomplished this by acting on behalf of both Crassus and Pompey's interests. He also tied himself through marriage alliances. Despite his familiarity and purported friendliness with both men, it was above all a political alliance — from which Caesar had gained the most. The death of Pompey's beloved Julia in 54 BC began to drive a wedge between the friendship that had been shared by both Caesar and Pompey. It created a gap that was beginning to seem irreconcilable, and severed the familial ties that had united the two despite Caesar and Pompey's best attempts to repair it.

Crassus' death therefore brought great concern to Pompey, who now was left behind as the sole counterweight to Caesar's burgeoning reputation. While Caesar was in Gaul and Crassus in Syria, Pompey remained in Rome, and defended the Triumvirate's interests in the face of what appeared to be increasing self-serving behavior on its part. The death of Crassus and the loss of the seven Legionary Eagles at Carrhae created turmoil for the Triumvirate as their opponents emerged from the everywhere to attack their policies. Chief among these voices was that of Clodius, who still persisted in 53 BC to be a nuisance for the Triumvirate. Milo's grant of street gangs by Pompey had only exacerbated the enmity he had for Clodius, and their rivalry for control of the Roman streets grew ever more bloody and out of control. What had begun as petty gang warfare was in danger of becoming an open war. In place of armed mobs, the rival elites now had trained gladiators in their entourage who were tasked with acting as bodyguards. Moreover, they represented the interests of thousands of poorer Romans, who came to be seen as a faction. While Milo ran for the consulship of 53 BC, Clodius in turn ran for the praetorship. Each tried to sabotage the other, until the violence became so extreme that the election had to be stalled until the following year. Shortly in 52 BC, both Milo and Clodius and their related entourages met one another by chance upon the Appian Way south of Bovillae. What began as a tense encounter was seemingly defused as the enemies began to go their separate ways, until the final members of each group broke into an altercation along the road. This small scuffle quickly grew into an open battle as one another's gladiators began to fight. The fighting was fierce and dirty — each side playing to underhanded tactics in an attempt to get the better of the other. The fighting concluded only when Clodius was struck by a stray dart, and forced to flee to the safety of a nearby inn for refuge. Milo ordered that his men follow Clodius and finish his political rival off. In a bout of cold blood, Clodius was murdered where he lay, and the slaves under his protection either killed or driven off into the surrounding woods. Although Clodius was killed, his wife still lived on. She served as a banner around which his supporters could rally. Using her late husband's reputation, she assembled her supporters and used their substantial numbers to establish Clodius' funeral pyre within the Roman senate house itself. The fires created by the pyre raged out of control, and consumed the entirety of the *Curia Hostilia* — a fitting final sendoff for a man who had been so strongly opposed to the monopolization of senatorial power while he lived.

The razing of the *Curia Hostilia* resulted in the Senate granting Pompey the consulship without a colleague. Such an appointment reveals the nature of the emergency in Rome, and the desperation with which the Senate tried to bring peace to the turmoil in the city. Pompey reacted to Clodius' supporters with a ruthless efficiency: he brought in loyal soldiers to attend every judicial and legislative process so as to prevent their interference. Moreover, he reformed Roman law to include new stipulations regarding electoral bribery and violence. Using these new laws, he then charged Milo, and betrayed his former ally. It was an act that intended to placate Clodius' supporters. This is revealed by the fact that Pompey himself had handpicked the jury. Furthermore, the presiding magistrate was Lucius Domitius Ahenobarbus, his client. Still, the mob persisted. During Cicero's defense of Milo for his charge of bribery, Pompey had to bring in armed legionaries to quiet the riotous crowd. Cicero, the greatest orator of the Republic, was so intimidated by the show of force by both factions that he was not capable of delivering his defense of the man. The trial resulted with Milo being exiled to Masillia.

While Caesar fought Vercingetorix in Gaul, Pompey began to make alliances with his fellow Triumvir's enemies. Caesar was aware now that his former ally was beginning to maneuver against him. In an attempt to win him back, Caesar offered his grandniece, Octavia, to Pompey for marriage. It was an offer that was refused. With Julia and Crassus dead, Pompey was alone in Rome and susceptible to coercion on the part of the *optimates*. They spoke to him as if they were longtime friends, whispering of Caesar's plans to remove Pompey from power once he had returned to Gaul. His former enemies spoke of the former triumphs enjoyed by Pompey, how Rome's greatest commander had fallen behind the successes achieved by the younger *Julii* upstart. The *optimates* convinced Pompey that he had been misled and used by Caesar, who they said intended to seize the Republic for himself. Their poisonous words were successful in their attempt at tearing the fabric of the Triumvirate. While Caesar brought Vercingetorix and the entirety of Gaul to heel upon the battlefield at Alesia, Pompey married himself to Cornelia Metella, the daughter of Caecilius Metellus Scipio: a fierce enemy of Caesar's. It was a gesture that could only be interpreted as hostile to Caesar's cause. Further alienating himself from the bonds of the Triumvirate, Pompey approved of a law that permitted retroactive prosecution for acts of electoral bribery. Such a law would make Caesar a client for prosecution once his grant of *imperium* came to a close. Caesar was furious about the betrayal. He knew that it was his enemies — the *optimates* — who were behind Pompey's sudden change in heart. He became determined to destroy the recent legislation passed by Pompey. However, every attempt of his was waylaid by Pompey's sweeping powers as singular consul. When Caesar attempted to stand for consul in *absentia* — being absent from Rome — his request was denied, despite the precedents that decreed that such a bid for office was permitted within the Roman system.

Each of Pompey's pieces of legislation was clearly oriented against Caesar. It had only been three years since the Lucca Conference, and already every one of Caesar's fears was proving itself true. Caesar's position in Gaul both preserved and robbed him of any opportunity to enact lasting change on legislation in Rome. He was powerless to curtail the efforts that sought to undermine his powerbase. With Crassus and Clodius dead, and Milo exiled to Masillia, Caesar had effectively been rendered feeble in Rome. The city had become a bastion for both Pompeian and *optimates*' forces. Pompey was little more than a tool to them, and acted against his former friend on behalf of their interests. They convinced him by feeding Pompey's ego and shoring up the insecurities that had emerged in light of Caesar's slew of Gallic victories. Cicero remarked how far the great general had fallen, how his diminished stature was the result of his inner turmoil at having to betray his former friend and ally. The oligarchy of the *optimates* would not relent, however. They demanded that

Caesar account for the crimes and injustices he had committed against them — the very same injustices they would have committed against him had the tables been reversed. In 51 BC, Pompey decreed that Caesar could not stand for consul unless he relinquished control of the armies he commanded in Gaul. Such a request was impossible for Caesar to comply with, as doing so would deprive himself of any protection against his enemies. In 50 BC, Caesar had concluded the five years that marked his term as governor of the Gallic provinces. Cicero aptly summarized the situation: "Pompey is determined that Caesar shall not become consul unless he hands over his army and provinces; Caesar is convinced that he will never be safe if he relinquishes his army." Evidently, with the absence of reconciliation between him and Pompey, there remained but one option left for Caesar to pursue — the path of war.

That these two men should come to blows was inevitable. Gaius Julius Caesar had done his utmost to stave off the possibility of an open conflict with Gnaeus Pompey Magnus to the extent of joining families with the man through marriage. As such, the death of Julia was a regrettable occurrence, and the rejection of Octavia an even more lamentable one. However, Pompey had shown his true colors. The successes Caesar had earned for himself over his enemies in Gaul had made him the envy of Rome. Marcus Licinius Crassus had sailed to the shores of the known world in search of wars in which he could compete with Caesar, and had gotten himself killed in its pursuit. With the West pacified, and the Eastern provinces in a state of flux, there was nowhere for Pompey to turn for conquests. A renewed war with Parthia would not be possible at any time in the near future. The *optimates* spied this defect in Pompey's character and coaxed it. They spoke adulations about Pompey's former successes, and eyed carefully the enigma on the horizon who was Caesar. Their primary goal in this was to disrupt the alliance that had come to dominate the decade. By dismantling the Triumvirate, political power would again be spread across the Senate's traditional powerbase, instead of being consolidated within the hands of a few. Once dissolved, the *optimates* could work on changing the legislation that had been enacted during the Triumvirate. Popular support was divided on the issue. Much of the Roman public regarded Pompey with the respect deserving of a hero of the Republic — a man who had conquered and done much for the people of Rome. However, the rapid success achieved by Julius Caesar had made him the man of the hour. In but a few short years, Caesar had accomplished the impossible. Through crude diplomacy and martial supremacy, Caesar had demonstrated his military genius and brought the entire Celtic dominance of Gaul to an end. Because of his efforts, Rome no longer had to fear the wrath of Celtic and Germanic tribes invading from beyond the Alps. Although only some in Rome loved Caesar, all respected him. Pompey was sick with envy. We must not forget that this was the same man who had attempted to rob Crassus of his glory following the Third Servile War. The gentle coaxing of the *optimates* was all that was necessary for him to begin to regard himself as the savior of the Republic. In passing the anti-bribery legislation on their behalf, he was himself fulfilling his own sordid fantasy of seeing his former ally brought low. The humiliation of the law courts, combined with its attack on a man's reputation, was enough to put the oligarchy of the *optimates* and Caesar at an impasse. Caesar demanded to be treated with the respect due to a man of his station, and the Senate refused to grant him it.

Left with no other diplomatic options to pursue, he turned instead to the very origin from where his power was rooted: his legions. Caesar was beloved by his soldiers. Having led them to countless spectacular victories over a myriad of enemies, they were prepared to follow him into one last conflict. Caesar could ask for no more of his men: they were fanatically devoted to his cause. With his tenth legion in tow, Caesar set his eyes southwards to Rome. There were his people; there sat Pompey; there ruled the corrupt oligarchy that had opportunistically asserted itself as the head of the state. 59 BC had marked the beginning of something new: an unofficial alliance between three men to share the power of the Roman state. This alliance had carried the Roman people to new heights through their defining conquests of the First Century BC. It had also brought them to new lows — defeats unseen since the days of Hannibal — upon the sands of Mesopotamia. Most days, blood flowed through the streets of Rome. But what started as a rule of three swiftly became unsustainable. Too many senators had a stake in the performance of power in Rome, and each continued to vie with the other for an increased control of the leadership. These third parties whispered poisonous words into the ears of the Triumvirs, seeking to divide them. To Caesar, such divisions had become apparent as early as the Luca Conference in 55 BC. It was evident that men of tremendous success and renown could not agree to share power for long. He was wary of intrigue, wary that his colleagues might attempt to oust him from power. He knew that the Triumvirate could not last forever. He knew that there could only be Caesar. So he prepared, waiting in Gaul for the opportune moment to strike. That the blow should fall on Pompey was a regrettable occurrence, but there remained the possibility that he could bring his friend back from the clutches of the *optimates*.

In 49 BC, Caesar and his solitary legion crossed the Rubicon River — the sacred boundary in which no armies under command were permitted to cross. To do so without relinquishing one's *imperium* was an act of unforgivable treason against the Roman people, and marked one an enemy of the Roman state. His life was forfeit; his right to property was void. The same would apply to his family: his grandniece Octavia, his grandnephew Octavius — all endangered by his actions. Caesar knew these risks, and yet he waded through the river's shallows regardless. His goal was the liberation of the Roman state from the *optimates*, and he was prepared to halt at nothing to bring himself to victory over the miserable charade of a Senate. Rome needed internal stability now more than ever if it was to maintain its hold on the vast dominions and provinces it now controlled. Its Republican system of government had been outgrown. To guarantee the wellbeing of the Roman state, a new form of government was necessary — one led by a strong man: an *imperator*. *"Alea Iacta Esto"* he said as he traversed. "Let the die be cast."

The Caesarian Civil War

Caesar's entrance into Italy was immediate, but merciful. He wanted to appear to the people of Italy as a great liberator rather than the tyrant that the Senate had portrayed him as. Pompey had earlier boasted that if he stamped his feet in Italy, legions would swarm to his call. However, he now found it difficult to rally enough soldiers to withstand Caesar's march on Rome, and himself and his allies being forced to abandon the city of Rome to their enemy. They fled south, with Caesar in pursuit, who only stopped briefly in Rome to quell the riotous mobs that had seized the city in the absence of Pompey. Pompey's march south had brought him near cities that contained clients of both he and his allies, and he found his army bolstered by additional soldiers. Despite these new numbers, Pompey still had little confidence in the army he led. He was desperate to make his way to Spain, the province in which enjoyed an esteemed reputation. Having governed the province for the better part of a decade, Pompey could draw on the populace there for a dependable supply of veterans. Caesar was aware of this possibility, and decided that Pompey was to be deprived of such manpower. Leaving his lieutenant, Marc Antony, in command of public order in Rome, Caesar mustered the entirety of his legions in Transalpine Gaul before leading his troops towards Spain. He arrived there at an astonishing speed, having completed the forced march in only 28 days. Pompey was bewildered: he had expected Caesar journey to take much longer because of his opponent's lack of naval transport. As a result, his defenses were inadequately prepared for Caesar's arrival, and his clients were taken by surprise. Spain was where the first major battle of the Caesarian Civil War occurred, with Caesar defeating a number of Pompey's lieutenants who were tasked with overseeing the province.

Having shown both his supremacy of Spain in addition to depriving Pompey of its resources, Caesar began to march eastward towards the province of Illyricum. There, Pompey was gaining a tremendous amount of leverage amidst the Roman and Greek communities. Through popular appeal to these cities, Pompey was swiftly expanding the ranks of the Senatorial army. This was of great concern to Caesar, who had presided over the province of Illyricum as consul and propraetor for the past ten years. He depended upon both it and the Gallic provinces for support. It was necessary that Caesar inflict a decisive defeat upon the Senatorial forces. This would convince the people of Italy that his cause was the just one. He decided to invade Illyricum, despite having inadequate vessels to transport the entirety of his army simultaneously. Hedging his bets, Caesar split his army in two and transported one half at a time. He made landfall with the first half after having run the enemy blockade in the winter of 48 BC. However, treacherous seas and an increased number of blockading vessels rendered it impossible for the second half of the army to follow through. Caesar was caught in a difficult position. He was trapped on the coast of Illyricum with no means of reaching the second half of his army. Divided, he knew he would prove easy prey for Pompey. Moreover, he was low on supplies and had no logistics support from the Italian mainland. Nor was he capable of asking local Greek or Italian settlements for aid, as they had already pledged themselves to

Pompey. What was necessary was that his second half make landfall in Illyricum, and soon. This was accomplished in the early summer of 48 BC. Led by Marc Antony, his forces were successful in penetrating the Senate's blockade and making landfall north of Caesar's camp. Pompey hastened to meet Antony before Caesar could reach them, but arrived too late to battle Caesar's reinforcements. Fearing that he might be caught in a vice grip between both armies, Pompey retreated to the nearby city of Dyrrachium, which allowed Caesar to consolidate his armies.

What ensued was a lengthy siege in which Caesar invested Dyrrachium for the entirety of the summer. Dyrrachium was founded amidst a mountain range, with its back accessible only by sea. This combination of elevation and remoteness made it a challenging fortress to besiege, as it was constantly capable of being resupplied from the ocean. Moreover, Caesar was incapable of preventing this, as he could not contest Pompey's naval superiority. Aware that a frontal assault would be catastrophic for his armies, Caesar chose to encircle the city with a wall of fortifications similar to those constructed at Alesia in 52 BC. Pompey was aware of Caesar's plan and did not stand idly by. What resulted was a race in which both sides built their own fortifications. In so doing, Pompey prevented Caesar from erecting his palisades close enough to the city to encompass it satisfactorily. A no-man's land emerged in the space between both sets of fortifications, within which fierce fighting occurred. Caesar knew that it was only a matter of time before Pompey would break, as the sheer number of Pompeian soldiers would greatly strain the city's supplies. Pompey was concerned of this. With the coming of fall, the harvest in the surrounding fields around Dyrrachium would occur, allowing Caesar to prolong his siege. He needed to strike, and soon. Defecting soldiers from Caesar's line informed Pompey of a weakness in Caesar's fortifications nearest the sea. With this in mind, Pompey organized an attack on Caesar's palisades. With six legions attacking the weak point alone, Pompey was capable of overwhelming Caesar's solitary ninth legion, which had been tasked with its protection. Despite being desperately outnumbered, the ninth legion stood firm, and allowed Caesar the chance to reinforce them with an additional 4,000 men. This attack was successful in repelling the Pompeian forces. However, their initial momentum came to a halt as they learned of just how outnumbered they truly were. There were roughly 45,000 Pompeian soldiers at Dyrrachium, compared to the 15,000 under Caesar. Caesar tried everything to gain leverage over his opponent. He concentrated his siege weapon fire to weaken the enemy ranks. Despite however many scorpion bolts were flung at Pompey's army, it showed no sign of abating. Pressed against such overwhelming odds, Caesar was forced to withdraw from his siege of Dyrrachium. The retreat soon broke into an all-out rout as Caesar's soldiers scrambled to escape. Rather than capitalize on the breaking of

Caesar's ranks, Pompey ordered a halt to the pursuit, fearing a trap. He believed that he had decisively beaten Caesar at Dyrrachium, and that soon his opponent would surrender. This proved to be far from the truth. Now in a position of weakness, Caesar captured a number of Illyrian cities to allow his soldiers the opportunity to rest and compose themselves. He knew that by allowing Pompey to use his sheer numbers in a siege, the battle would only result in a defeat. He needed to draw Pompey out onto an open field.

Only weeks after the disaster at Dyrrachium, Caesar mobilized his soldiers and marched them to Pharsalus in Thessaly. At Pharsalus, Pompey had every advantage. He possessed superiority in numbers, with his legions being full-strength and numbering some 45,000 men. Furthermore, he had stable supply lines, as the numerous nearby Greek cities were each subservient to his cause. Caesar, on the other hand, only led 22,000 men. These were all soldiers who were fiercely loyal to his cause, but each legion was depleted in numbers. Moreover, Caesar was operating in enemy country. Being in central Greece, he was effectively isolated from Italy, with no hope of receiving reinforcements at this point. Pompey knew this, which prompted him to act more conservatively. He wanted to spend the entirety of August besieging Caesar in his camp, and negating any possibility for his opponent to resupply. He believed that this would force Caesar's hand and result in a full surrender of his army. The *optimates* had different hopes in mind. They desired a decisive victory, one that would symbolically demonstrate their superiority over Caesar and undermine his powerbase throughout Italy. As a result, they chastised Pompey for choosing to meekly pursue a war of attrition. Pompey, ever their puppet, decided to pursue the *optimates* plan and engage Caesar in pitched battle. This would prove his undoing.

The Pompeian forces were arranged in the traditional *triplex acies*, with the most experienced veterans being posted on the flanks. His center was commanded by Scipio, and comprised of the Syrian legions. His right flank was protected by the Enipeius River, which allowed him to concentrate the entirety of his cavalry on one flank. Pompey's plan was to overwhelm the numerically inferior Caesarian cavalry, and then strike at Caesar's lines from the rear while his infantry engaged the front.

Caesar knew that surrendering to the Senate was no longer an option, and that defeat at Pharsalus would mean death for himself and all of his men. The loyalty of his men was reinforced by this knowledge, and they stood by their commander with a dedication that other Roman generals could only dream of. He deployed his army in a similar manner as Pompey's, weighing the entirety of his cavalry on one flank against his adversary's. He deliberately thinned the depth of his ranks so as to allow for the possibility of a hidden fourth rank, with which he could support his own cavalry in their engagement. He personally led the cavalry, and trusted his centurions to command the infantry cohorts in battle. These were grizzled veterans who were experienced from a decade of vicious fighting with the Gauls. Disciplined and skilled warriors, Caesar's legions could operate with a certain degree of autonomy that did not sacrifice the greater cohesion of the army. Caesar praised this characteristic of his soldiers, believing it maximized their effectiveness. They marched the great distance that separated their host from Pompey, and halted just short of the enemy lines to rest and recover. Pompey's soldiers dared not move — a questionable decision, given how Caesar's army was momentarily vulnerable. The heavy infantry collided, Caesarian legionaries stabbing and bashing at Pompeian legionaries as each desperately tried to best the other. The extensive experience of Caesar's men adequately made up for their lack in numbers. They tore into the enemy ranks, which prompted Pompey to issue the order for his cavalry to attack. As expected, the Pompeian cavalry was getting the better of their Caesarian counterpart until Caesar gave the order for the fourth rank to come into action. The fourth rank reserves charged, stabbing and hewing at the horses with their *pilas* with such ferocity that the Pompeian cavalry was forced to rout. Witnessing his cavalry crumble before him, Pompey fled the battlefield for his camp, abandoning his soldiers to their fates. Caesar then issued the command that the reserves and cavalry were to envelop the Pompeian ranks. Being covered by enemies from all sides, the Pompeian army quickly abandoned hope and fled. Having suffered a paltry few losses, Caesar gave orders that his victorious soldiers were to assault and plunder the enemy camp. His men threw themselves at the walls and parapets that defended the Senate's camp, and cut down the auxiliaries who were tasked with its defense. Within it they found much treasure and plunder, but neither Pompey nor any of the *optimates* were anywhere to be found. All had fled.

Pharsalus was the deciding event of the Caesarian Civil War. Upon its fields, a significantly smaller Caesarian force had triumphed over its Pompeian counterpart. It was a catastrophic defeat for the *optimates*: several thousand of their soldiers had been killed compared to a few hundred losses suffered by Caesar. The senators were forced to flee from the site of the battle, abandoning everything they owned in an attempt to find refuge at the distant corners of the dominion. Pompey himself fled to Egypt, hoping to find safety in the court of the Ptolemies. Caesar followed in hot pursuit. Contrary to what might be expected, Caesar did not desire vengeance on Pompey. He understood that his friend had been deceived and led astray by the *optimates*. Even though Pompey had raised armies to combat him, he was merciful. He granted amnesty to the majority of his opponents in the Senate. What he desired most was the resolution of conflict between himself and Pompey, and for his friend to return home. However, upon arrival in Egypt, Pompey was assassinated under order of the Pharaoh Ptolemy XIII. Ptolemy XIII had misunderstood Caesar. He believed that in murdering Pompey he would be placing himself in Caesar's good graces. The very opposite occurred. Infuriated by the callousness of Ptolemy's presumptions and driven by despair, Caesar created an alliance with Ptolemy's sister, Cleopatra VII, and assisted her in usurping her brother's throne. In this way, Egypt was brought finally into the Roman Empire.

With Gnaeus Pompey Magnus' death in Egypt, the era of the Triumvirate had come to an end. Gaius Julius Caesar, despite his best attempts, had been incapable of rescuing his former friend from the clutches of the *optimates*. What resulted was a difficult struggle between the two factions in which much Roman blood was spilled. When the dust and smoke of the Caesarian Civil War cleared, it became apparent to all that Caesar had triumphed. Although he granted amnesty to his former enemies, it was obvious that they were subservient to his wishes. In 45 BC, Caesar was master of the Senate, and the entirety of Rome. As reward for his merciful behavior, the Senate appointed him dictator. The senators also pardoned his crimes, and forgave him for the prior instances of electoral bribery. The Roman public loved him. He threw extravagant games, and celebrated his triumphal victories over the Gauls and Egyptians. He had both Vercingetorix and the Egyptian queen, Arsinoe IV, paraded through the streets of Rome. As dictator, he passed a great deal of legislation that was designed to bring stability and peace to the Italian peninsula. He rewarded families that had a great number of children, and outlawed the political clubs that had previously been used by Clodius and Milo to create so much chaos and violence in the streets of Rome. He personally financed the reconstruction of many parts of the city that had been damaged by the incessant conflict of the first century. With Gaius Julius Caesar at the helm, it seemed that the Roman people could look forward to peace for the first time in a long time.

Other books available by author on Kindle, paperback and audio:

The Second Triumvirate of Rome:
Augustus, Mark Antony, Marcus Aemilius Lepidus, And The Founding Of An Empire

Bibliography

<u>Primary Sources</u>

Appian, *Civil Wars*, trans. Lacus Curtius. Accessible at:

http://penelope.uchicago.edu/Thayer/E/Roman/Texts/Appian/Civil_Wars/1*.html

Caesar, *Civil Wars,* trans. MIT. Accessible at:

http://classics.mit.edu/Caesar/civil.1.1.html

Caesar, *Gallic Wars,* trans. MIT. Accessible at:
http://classics.mit.edu/Caesar/gallic.html

Cicero, *Pro Cluentio*, trans. Perseus. Accessible at:
http://www.perseus.tufts.edu/hopper/text?doc=Cic.clu

Cicero, *Pro Roscio*, trans. Perseus. Accessible at:

http://www.perseus.tufts.edu/hopper/text?doc=Cic.rosc

Cicero, *Pro Plancio*, trans. Perseus. Accessible at:

http://www.perseus.tufts.edu/hopper/text?doc=
Cic.plan

Cicero, *Letters to Atticus*, trans. Perseus. Accessible at:

http://data.perseus.org/texts/urn:cts:latinLit:ph
i0474.phi057.perseus-lat1

Livy, *History of Rome*, trans. Perseus. Accessible at:
http://www.perseus.tufts.edu/hopper/text?doc=
Liv.

Plutarch, *Roman Lives,* trans. MIT. Accessible at:

http://classics.mit.edu/Browse/index-
Plutarch.html

Polybius, *The Histories,* trans. Lacus Curtius. Accessible at:

http://penelope.uchicago.edu/Thayer/E/Roman
/Texts/Polybius/3*.html

Tacitus, *Historia,* Book 3, trans. Lacus Curtius. Accessible at:

http://penelope.uchicago.edu/Thayer/E/Roman/Texts/Tacitus/Histories/3B*.html

Secondary Sources

Ewins, U. "The Early Colonization of Cisalpine Gaul" in *Papers of the British School at Rome, vol. 20* (1952), pp. 54-71. Retrieved from http://www.jstor.org/stable/40310497

Ewins, U. "The Enfranchisement of Cisalpine Gaul" in *Papers of the British School at Rome, vol. 23* (1955), pp. 73-98. Retrieved from http://www.jstor.org/stable/40310532

Granovetter, M. "The Strength of Weak Ties: A Network Theory Revisited" in *Sociological Theory, vol. 1* (1983), pp. 201-233. Retrieved from http://www.jstor.org/stable/202051

Guidobaldi, M. "Transformations and continuities in a conquered territory: The case of the Ager Praetutianus," in Keay, S. and Terranto, N. (eds.) *Italy and the West: Comparative Issues in Romanization* (Oxford: Oxbow Books, 2009), pp. 85-90.

Keay, S. "Coastal Communities of Hisapania Citerior" in Blagg, T. and Millet, M. (eds.) *The Early Roman Empire in the West* (Oxford: Oxbow Books, 2002) p. 120-150.

Lomas, K. "The Weakest Link: Elite Social Networks in Republican Italy" in S.T. Roselaar (ed.), *Processes of integration and identity formation in the Roman Republic: 197-214.* (Leiden, Brill. 2012), pp. 199-213.

McDonald, A. H. "The Roman Conquest of Cisalpine Gaul (201-191 B.C.)" in *Antichthon, 8*,44. (1974) Retrieved from http://search.proquest.com/docview/13000922 65?accountid=12339

Millett, M. "Romanization: Historical Issues and Archaeological Interpretation" in Blagg, T. and Millet, M. (eds.) *The Early Roman Empire in the West* (Oxford: Oxbow Books, 2002) p. 35-41.

Mouritsen, H. "The Making of the Italian Question: The Ancient Tradition of the Social War" in Mouritsen, H. (ed.) *Italian Unification: A study in Ancient and Modern Historiography* (London: University of London Press, 1998). p. 4-143.

Patterson, J. "The Relationship of the Italian Ruling Classes with Rome: Friendship, Family Relations and Their Consequences" in Jehne/Pfeilschifter (eds.), *Herrschaft und Integration? Rom und Italien in republikanischer Zeit* (2006) 139-153.

Purcell, N. "The Creation of Provincial Landscape: the Roman Impact on Cisalpine Gaul" in Blagg, T. and Millet, M. (eds.) *The Early Roman Empire in the West* (Oxford: Oxbow Books, 2002) pp. 7-29.

Rees, W. "'Ex Italia convenerunt' (Cic. Dom. 12.30): Italian Participation in Roman Political Life (133-44 BC)" in Keaveney, A. and Earnshaw-Brown, L. (eds.) *The Italians on the Land: Changing Perspectives on Republican Italy Then and Now* (Cambridge: Cambridge Scholars Publishing, 2009), pp. 85-101.

Roselaar, S., "Colonies and processes of integration in the Roman Republic" en *Mélanges de l'École française de Rome - Antiquité* [En ligne], *vol.123,* no. 2 (2011), pp. 527-555. Mis en ligne le 19 février 2013, consulté le 12 décembre 2014. URL : http://mefra.revues.org/445

Terrenato, N. "Tam firmum municipium: the Romanization of Volaterrae and its Cultural Implication" in *JRS, vol.* 99 (1998), pp.94-114.

Ventura, P. et al. "Aquileia: a crossroad of men and ideas" in *Romanization und Resistenz in Plastik, Architektur und Inschriften der Provinzen des Imperium Romanum: neue Funde und Forschungen / herausgegeben von Peter Noelke mit Friederike Naumann-Steckner und Beate Schneider* (Mainz: P. Von Zabern, 2003), pp. 651-667.

Williams, J.H.C. "Roman Intentions and Romanization: Republican Northern Italy, c. 200-100 BC" in Keay, S. and Terranto, N. (eds.) *Italy and the West: Comparative Issues in Romanization* (Oxford: Oxbow Books, 2009), pp. 91-101.

38724440R00142

Made in the USA
Middletown, DE
10 March 2019